Becoming

Jim Branch

For my dear Carol, the love of my life. Every time I think that I couldn't possibly love you more than I do at this minute, you prove me wrong once again. I love you.

~Jim

Contents:

Preface

Socrates once said, "The only true wisdom is in knowing you know nothing." I totally get that, because no matter how much I may think I know at times, and no matter how often the voices within and around me might try to convince me otherwise, I always come back to the same realization, "I really don't know anything." I'm only just beginning to scratch the surface of this infinitely deep mystery that we call God. There is always so much more of Him, so much more to learn and to know than I can ever begin to fathom in a multitude of lifetimes. And that, believe it or not, is a great place to be. And it also may be the best place possible for beginning a book.

That is not an attempt to minimize what you hold in your hands, or what you will read in the pages that follow. It is simply a confession that the more of God I come to know, the more I realize what I don't know. This book was a long time in the making. It is the attempt to verbalize a journey that has taken place over the span of thirty-plus years of following Jesus, as well as the words and wisdom that has been invested in me by numerous saints, poets and pilgrims during that time. This book is an account of my experience of being drawn closer and closer to God's heart by the work of his Spirit within me.

Thus, the pages that follow are not a magic formula, or words of wisdom, or seven steps to anything in particular; they are just the ramblings that go on inside my heart and soul on a regular basis as I think about the life of God within me and how that life has grown and been nurtured through the years. It is only my story, and I don't assume that it is anyone else's, but if there is something in my story that helps you make some sense of your own, then I am extraordinarily grateful. Thank you for your willingness to join me on this adventure.

Introduction

This is a book about words. I know, I know, every book is about words, right? But that's not really what I mean. This book is not just a book containing words, it is a book about words. And not just any words, but words that have been friends and companions; guides within me for some time now. This book is about words that have been planted deeply in the soil of my soul and have taken root there, and have begun to produce some sort of fruit — although I can't fully tell exactly what kind of fruit that may be.

Words, by their very nature, have life within them — they contain the power to create. I think this is true because the origin of words — their true source — is *the* Word. For whenever and wherever *the* Word is spoken, things come to be; both around us and within us. Haven't we all experienced the beauty of this process at one time or another when *the* Word was spoken to us and resonated deeply within us? It is almost as if some kind of chord is struck inside us that we didn't fully know was there — resulting in something new being created, or awakened. Something comes alive within us that, quite simply, was not alive before.

And because words hold this amazing and mysterious power — the power of God's Spirit — they are something to be cherished and treasured, as well as something to be wisely used and dearly held. Maybe that's why I have loved words for as long as I can remember.

This book is about words; six of them to be exact. They are words that have formed a bit of a framework for the life of God within me: words that offer rich images to step into, words that provide a certain rhythm to move to, words that invite us to a window through which we can get a better view of God, and life, and faith. They are words that share a connectedness that allows us to see, and better understand, the connectedness of all things. And, finally, they are words that move in a particular direction, leading us toward a much desired destination — that of spiritual transformation.

These six words are: *recognize, release, receive, believe, rest,* and *become.* Four of the six are right out of the pages of *the* Word: *"He was in the world, and though the world was made through him, the world did not* **recognize** *him. He came to that which was his own, but his own did not* **receive** *him. Yet to all who* **received** *him, to those who* **believed** *in his name, he gave the right to* **become** *children of God — children born not of natural descent, nor of human decision or a husband's will, but born of God." (John 1:10-12).* And the other two have been identified by the saints and the poets throughout the centuries in describing the process of spiritual formation: *release, receive, rest,* which are my blue-collar version of the words purgation, illumination, and union. But regardless of where they come from, they have been words of life to me; words that have pointed me in the direction of the spiritual transformation I most deeply long for.

And isn't that, in our heart of hearts, what we all truly desire? Don't we all have a deep longing for true and lasting change — for genuine spiritual transformation? We might not always be aware of it, but it is there. We all yearn to be all that we were created to be when *the Dreamer first dreamt us into being* (thank you Robert Benson).

And it doesn't take a genius to figure out that all of us — myself much more than most — fall woefully short of that image on a pretty regular basis. What we really desire is a life of substance and depth, which is lived from a place of integrity and truth. We long for a life in which we love deeply and are deeply loved. How exactly to accomplish all of this, we have no idea most of the time, but it is what we all most deeply long for. And that is exactly what this book is about. As I said before, it is not a formula or a "how to," but rather a collection of thoughts about words that seem to move — or at least seemed to have moved me — in that general direction.

Chapter One

Recognize

rec·og·nize [rek-*uh* g-nahyz]: to perceive as existing or true.

He was in the world, and though the world was made through him, the world did not **recognize** *him. (John 1:10)*

Okay, let's get this out of the way right off the bat. I have a confession to make: I am a huge college football fan. I don't know, maybe it started when my folks took me to see my first college game when I was seven years old. Or maybe it was the numerous Saturdays afterwards when I had the privilege of traveling to stadiums all over the southeast watching some of the best football to be seen. Maybe it's the passion, maybe it's the excitement, maybe it's the tradition, or the pageantry; who really knows? All I know is that throughout my lifetime—and yes even to this day—if I am not watching a game in person on a fall Saturday, I am glued to the television from dawn to dusk watching every act of this great American drama.

Needless to say, my family didn't come through this experience unfazed. My kids grew up tailgating, watching the band march by playing our favorite fight song, and enduring heat and rain and wind and cold to cheer on our beloved team, in victory and in defeat. In fact, some of my very best memories revolve around some part of this "dance" as it was played out on some particular Saturday, in one game or another—but that's for another book.

One day, when my youngest son was eight or nine, my father and I decided to take him to his first "road game." We decided to make it a true *road trip* and allow him to make almost all of the decisions about where we would eat, what we would do, when we would stop, etc. The game was about three hours away, which seemed like the perfect distance to feel like we were really traveling, but not killing ourselves to do it. And perfect, it seemed, for a kid his age—

he would love it. And love it he did! It was everything we hoped it would be: a beautiful (if not absolutely freezing) late November day, an exciting game (eventually won by the good guys), sitting right beside the band amidst all the other fans of our beloved team. We couldn't have asked for anything more.

Very early in the first quarter, with the score tied at zero and the *bad guys* driving deep into our territory, my son turned to me and said, "Dad, could I get a Coke and some popcorn?" I'll have to admit, I was torn. Something significant was happening on the field, which is what I knew we had all come to see, and yet, hadn't I promised that this would be his day and that he would call most of the shots? So, with much reluctance I headed toward the concession stand.

As I was standing in line, waiting my turn to spend a small fortune on what at the grocery store would cost only a few dollars, there came an enormous cheer from the fans in our section. Apparently the *good guys* had done something just short of heroic in stopping the drive short of our goal line. As I walked toward the tunnel back to our seats — popcorn and Coke firmly in hand — I was greeted by a fellow fan who said simply, "That's the most amazing thing I've ever seen."

I re-entered the stadium just in time to see my son and my father jumping up and down cheering, high fiving, and singing the words to our favorite fight song as the band played on. And as I watched all of this unfold I thought, "I missed it. That was the whole reason we came here, to have moments just like that…together…all of us! And *I missed it* because I was standing in line for popcorn."

Kind of a strange way to start a book about the spiritual life, huh? But the fact of the matter is that this scene, even though it happened years ago, still lives on in my memory, continuing to linger in my heart and my soul since that day. Why? Probably because I feel that way about so many things in my life — particularly my spiritual life. I can so easily get distracted by circumstances, or busyness, or needs, or demands, that so often I look back on a day or an interaction or a conversation and think, *I missed it. God was there, and He was up to something, but I just wasn't paying attention.* An amazing opportunity to be a part of something transcendent was available and I was standing in line for popcorn.

You see, like many people (I suspect), I have a little trouble *recognizing*. And *recognizing* is such an important part of the spiritual life; recognizing what is going on within or beneath or beyond what we are able to see, and beginning to pay attention in such a way that we are actually able to *really see* both where God is present and what he is up to in the comings and the goings of our lives. But recognizing does not come automatically, it requires something of us. It requires us to stop living on the surface of things, to slow down enough to pay attention, to make space in our lives to reflect and to pray, and to train our souls — and thus our eyes — to look deeper into things.

Luckily, when it comes to my ability — or lack thereof — to *recognize* God in the midst of the craziness of life, I am not alone. It seems that many others have struggled with this exact thing. In fact, the Scriptures are absolutely full of stories where recognizing God was a key issue; be it *surely the Lord was in this place and I was not aware of it* (Genesis 28:16), or *then Eli realized that the Lord was calling the boy* (1 Samuel 3:8), or *at this, she turned around and saw Jesus standing there, but she did not realize that it was Jesus* (John 20:14), or *early in the morning, Jesus stood on the shore, but the disciples did not realize it* (John 21:4), or *were not our hearts burning within us while he spoke to us on the road* (Luke 24:32). All of these stories involve places where recognizing, be it in the midst of the encounter or after the fact, played a key role. So the question then becomes, how do I begin to cultivate and nurture a life of attentiveness to God, to His voice, and to His presence?

Slow Down

As fast as we spin around in our everyday lives, it is a wonder we can recognize anything, much less what is going on beneath the surface. Our lives get so busy and so chaotic, and the noise around and within us so loud, that it makes *recognizing* extraordinarily difficult; especially recognizing a God who often speaks in such a still, soft voice. Why is that? What is it that makes us cram our lives so incredibly full? Why are we so occupied — and even preoccupied — that it is next to impossible for anyone or anything, other than what is loudest and most demanding, to get our attention on any consistent basis? The answers to those questions, although difficult, are key to our ability (and even our desire) to dig our heels in against the speed of life, and begin to slow the wheels of progress — which in some weird way is actually what we believe it is — down a few miles per hour.

To answer these questions, we must start at the core. If we are really honest with ourselves, we will have to admit that our worth and value — our identity — is tied up in some terribly dysfunctional way with how much stuff we do, and how valuable we are to our world, whatever that world may be. In other words, somehow we have come to believe that we *are* what we *do*. And if we live by this mantra we will always be running around helter-skelter, like crazy people, because we can never quite do enough to feel really good about ourselves. We *need* to be needed, we *need* to be essential, we *need* our world to depend on us. We are very needy people, and as long as that is true, slowing down will never be a possibility. And as long as slowing down is not a possibility, living a life of attentiveness to God will not be a possibility either.

However, when we make the shift from trying to create our identity — making a name for ourselves, if you will — to receiving our worth and value (our identity) from God alone (which is discussed further in a later chapter) then we are free to put on the brakes when it comes to this life of out-of-control busyness. Slowing down actually becomes a possibility because we don't need anyone or anything else to define us. I must begin to realize that I am not essential; the world can in fact get by without me. And when I do slow down and become more present to God and to people, the world actually gets a much better *me* in the bargain. And I receive freedom: freedom from the demands of both my insecurity and my world; freedom from needing anyone or anything to define me or determine my worth; freedom to say "yes" and "no" as God directs, rather than as my fearful heart demands or determines.

Simply put, as we become more and more convinced of our value in Christ and in Christ alone, we find ourselves more able to slow down. And when we find ourselves more able to slow down, we become more open and attentive to the voice of God both within us and around us. Thus, we find ourselves not only more aware, but more at peace, and more able to pay attention. Or, as the name of the chapter states, more able to *recognize*.

What does this prying ourselves away from our *compulsive self* look like, practically speaking? That can differ dramatically from person to person, but here are a few things that have helped in my effort to slow down.

First of all, walk slower. I know, I know, sounds a little ridiculous, doesn't it? But it really helps. I have a friend who is a cardiologist, and one day he told another friend of ours a most amazing thing. He said that in emergency situations at the hospital, he trained himself to never run. When I heard this, I thought to myself: "What? Never run? When life and death is hanging in the balance?" And, lo and behold, that is the very reason for never running. There are plenty of people at the hospital trained to do the million and one things that must be done when an emergency occurs, but his job required something very particular. When he got in that room, he was going to be called upon to guide and direct, to make life or death decisions. Therefore, he needed to take his time getting to the scene, and make sure he was clear-minded, thoughtful, and composed once he arrived. The life of the patient depended on it. Most of us don't have life or death decisions hanging in the balance, but I think we will find that if we begin to walk slower (and driving slower can have the same effect), it will begin to change the very same things about us; making us more reflective, thoughtful, and composed as we go about the daily demands of our lives.

Next, eat slower. Some call this *savoring*. Savoring is a wonderful practice, and a bit of a lost art I'm afraid. Take time to enjoy the look and the smell of your food. Allow your mind and your heart to consider who prepared it for you, and where it came from. Let your soul be filled with gratitude for God's care and provision. Thank him for both.

Then enjoy the taste of your food. Chew it fully and drain every bit of flavor out of every single bite before you swallow. By doing this you will then be able to practice the art of savoring in other contexts — whether being with God, or sitting with friends, or having a great conversation, or watching a sunset. It will just begin to become a part of your life, and allow you to be more fully present and more fully engaged in each and every encounter.

Here's another one: go to the back of lines. Again, I know it sounds crazy, but a friend of mine once said that "if you ever want to find Jesus, just go to the back of the line" (rather than jockeying for position in the front). And you know what? He was right. Try it and you will see. There is just something about not trying to get to the front of a line that creates space, not only for God's Spirit within us, but also for great conversations among us. It opens our eyes both to God and to those we are in the midst of.

And the last thing is, learn to say *no*. Trying to please everyone all the time is an incredible burden to carry; and a burden that usually stems from sinful rather than noble purposes, if we're really honest. This is an area where our *compulsive self* can be hardest to identify and defeat. Both our world and our culture tell us to say *yes* to everything; the more the better. It is a terribly hard default mode to change.

But ultimately it is God alone to whom we must say *yes*; and then to other things only as a result of that ultimate *yes* to Him. It can be really confusing and really difficult to say *no* to the people — and the things — in our lives and world, unless we are well in tune with the voice of the One who called us to love him with all our heart, soul, mind, and strength, and then to love others as a result of that love for him.

Make Space

I was speaking to a group of college students a few years ago about living a life of depth and quality with God. One of the first things I told them was that if we want to live a life of intimacy and deep connectedness to God (in the beautiful words of Richard Foster), "It's not just going to fall on our heads. We must desire it and seek it out. We must order our lives in particular ways." In short, we must relentlessly make time and space for God every day.

Inevitably, in that type of conversation, *the* question then always arises: "How do you find time to do that? How do you find time to be with God each day?" And of course the answer is…you don't. You don't *find* time, you have to *make* time. If you're trying to *find* time, you will rarely if ever succeed. You must *make* it. By far the thing that has had the most dramatic impact on my spiritual life over the last 30+ years — that thing that God has used to shape and form and mold me probably more than any other — has been practicing this one simple thing. Make time and space for God every day. Be relentless about it. Guard it. Protect it. Fight for it. The quality of the life of God within you depends on it.

The truth is that we will make time for the things that we truly believe are most important. So maybe what we really need is to be more and more convinced of the importance of making space for God. Look no further than Luke 10:38-42. In this passage Jesus is as clear as he possibly could be about what is the most important thing.

The story of Mary and Martha is a classic example of the important versus the urgent. Martha has opened her home to Jesus and is busy scurrying around trying to get everything done; after all, preparations had to be made, right? But Martha is so busy making these preparations that she *misses it.* She misses the point, the whole reason she wanted to make the preparations in the first place — Jesus! In fact the word used to describe Martha's state of being is *distracted.*

The word distract comes from the Latin word *distractus,* which means to draw apart or away. Martha's attention had been drawn away by all the things *she thought* had to be done. The Greek word used here is *perispao,* which means *to drag around.* What a great description of what was going on within Martha, she was being dragged around. All of her agendas and plans — that were birthed out of her needs, fears, and insecurities — had created a sense of urgency within her that kept her from seeing and valuing what was more important at the moment. Jesus addresses this sense of urgency when he brings to her attention the fact that she is *worried and upset about many things;* or, more literally, *torn up about many things.*

Then, Jesus goes on to remind Martha that Mary had chosen what is best — the *good part* — and it would not be taken from her. The Message uses the word *essential* here; Mary had chosen what was essential. And what exactly had Mary chosen? She had chosen to *sit at Jesus' feet, listening to what he said.* That is the essential part! That is the important part! But, unfortunately, it is not usually the most urgent part.

I was having lunch with a very wise man years ago when he told me, "The quality of our lives will be determined by how well we do the things that are important, but not particularly urgent." He went on to explain that all of us have things to do that are urgent in nature; some of them important, and some merely urgent. *The key is to not allow the urgent but not important things to take our time away from the important but not urgent things.* What incredibly wise words;

words that Mary had learned the truth and value of firsthand. Jesus was present, and everything else would have to take a back seat to him. She would not allow the urgent things to drag her around, and away, from her beloved Jesus. Mary had taken a *posture* of sitting at his feet and made a *practice* of listening to what he had to say. And as a result her heart had been totally and completely captured with love for him. He was the most important thing. Wouldn't it be great if the rest of us could be as convinced of that as she was? How might that happen?

A friend once told me that if you want to be a good writer you have to *practice* making good sentences. It is an art, but it is also a discipline. It seems to me that's the way it is with just about anything in our lives that we would like to get better at. The best way to get better at something is to *practice* it. Therefore, if we are really serious about living a life at attention, a life aware and alert to the ways and the places and the people through which God is likely to show up, the best way we can begin to do that is to set aside some space and time each day for that express purpose; where we *practice* just that. We must consistently take the *posture* of sitting at his feet, and maintain the *practice* of listening to what he has to say.

Practical ways to do this involve treating our time with God as we would treat time with any other significant person in our lives — put it in our calendar, treat it as a nonnegotiable, be thoughtful and intentional about it, give it the best and most alert part of our day. If someone or something begins to infringe on or demand that time we say, "I have an appointment and am unavailable."

Also, set aside a particular place to be with God; a place where you can be alone and uninterrupted, a place where you can give your total attention to him. Let it be a place that brings you to life in a certain way. If you are most alive when you are outdoors, find a place outdoors. If you come to life in a place where there are meaningful symbols and visuals, find a chapel or sanctuary. If you are most alive in a comfortable, warm setting, find a favorite chair by a large window or fireplace. Place really does matter in the spiritual life, so be intentional about where you will be with God.

And, finally, have some structure, or an intentional plan, for your time with him. Structure does not hinder or cramp the work and movement of the Spirit within us; it actually does just the opposite. Just as a rose grows best on some kind of structure, so too do our spiritual lives. We need something to guide and direct, something to enable and nurture us to grow and to stretch the arms of our soul up toward the life-giving sun of God's presence. For years I have used various books to guide my time with God; always selecting one that points me to specific scripture each day that I can immerse myself in, one that calls me to set aside time to pray and reflect, to listen and to respond. The one that has been most helpful to me through the years has been *Disciplines for the Inner Life* by Bob Benson and Michael W. Benson. It gives me a worship service each day, with a Psalm and a scripture passage and prayers and readings — even a song — all gathered around a particular theme. For

years its gentle structure has brought me to life inside.
Structure brings life.

Be Quiet

It is impossible to underestimate the value of silence and
solitude in this process. The life of the Spirit within us just
seems to thrive on it, if not require it. Unfortunately, silence
and solitude are not a regular and normal part of our
everyday lives. Our world is filled with so much noise. And
when the noise on the outside finally dies away, we find that
we are filled with just as much noise on the inside. What are
we to do? How can we possibly hear anything, much less
the voice of the Spirit within us, who typically speaks in
such a soft tone? We must learn to be quiet, to still the outer
noise in such a way that it begins to help still the inner noise
as well. And then maybe, just maybe, after a little practice at
this "stilling" process, we will be able to hear the voice of
God within us.

Our souls are like the waters of a pond, many of the saints
and poets have told us. And when our world is noisy, it is
like the waters (our souls) are so stirred up and agitated that
it is impossible to see what is underneath. But when we
come to silence — which leads to stillness — the chaotic waters
begin to settle, and over time the waters become completely
calm. Then, and only then, are we able to see clearly what
lies beneath. Then, and only then, can we be attentive and
aware enough to really hear and really see whatever there is

to be heard and seen. Then, and only then, is *recognizing* a possibility.

"You don't have to sit outside in the dark," wrote Annie Dillard. "If however, you want to look at the stars, you will find that darkness is necessary. But the stars neither require nor demand it." Thus, "You don't have to sit in silence," a dear friend once told me, "but if you want to hear from God, you will find that silence is necessary." And I believe it. Furthermore, I have found it to be true time after time. If I am serious about living a life at attention, if I have a deep longing to consistently hear the voice of God in my life, if I have any hope of ever living a life where *recognizing* is a possibility, I must begin to practice silence and solitude in some kind of meaningful way. There is simply no way around it. Silence and solitude deepen the quality of our life with God.

Years ago I was taking a group of high school folks on a retreat for a time of guided silence and solitude. I had a friend that I deeply love and respect come to lead our time. I had wondered, honestly, what these high school friends would think about such a time; whether they would think it was totally weird or whether they would embrace it and be drawn into it. I found that they absolutely loved it; as a matter of fact they all recognized a deep need within themselves to listen and wait and simply be. It turns out that they didn't get that opportunity very often; most of their lives revolved around demands and performance.

As my friend led us through our first time together and into a time of silent reflection, he asked each of us to simply be still and let all of the noise and chaos stop for a moment. Then he asked each of us to listen. Listen to the Spirit of God deep within us. After we had spent a few minutes listening, he asked us to listen for one particular word that God might have for us as we began the retreat. And, with all eyes closed, he asked us to *recognize* that word and softly whisper it to God.

I have a confession to make. I never close my eyes during those moments. I like to see the faces of the people around me as they respond to whatever God might be doing within them. So, I watched as my friends softly uttered their words. What an incredibly sweet time it was to see; to see how God had met each one of these dear friends, and what word he had given them to utter back to him.

One high school friend in particular sat in silence with a growing grin on her face; almost as if God was slowly wooing her to himself during the time. As this dear one sat in this grin-filled silence, the grin began to grow into a full smile as she uttered softly her word…*sssshhhhh*. It was an absolutely beautiful moment to see. God had given this dear child of His, as well as myself, a sweet gift—the gift of being able *to be*.

Maybe your adventure into silence needs to start with a similar weekend. Or maybe you need to set aside a day a month to be with Him in silence for the entire day. Or maybe you need to set a particular time each day to simply sit before him in silence and stillness for a period of time— be it an hour or be it ten minutes. Or maybe you've been doing this for quite a while and have already found your way to integrate silence and solitude into the rhythm of your life. Whatever the case, let me just encourage you to start somewhere. Maybe you too will sit in a grin-filled silence and hear the invitation from your God to receive the gift that causes the deepest places in your soul simply to say…*ssssshhhhh*.

Practice

One particular way the saints throughout the centuries have encouraged fellow pilgrims in the art of recognition is called *examen*. It is a simple practice where we set aside time at the end of the day to take the hand of Jesus and allow him to silently and prayerfully walk us back through the moments and events of our day, allowing us to pay particular attention to its contents and conversations. As we go, we pay special attention to the things that either brought us life in some way, or that disturbed or disrupted us for some reason. What needs to be celebrated? What needs to be confessed? What needs to be savored or reflected upon further? The goal is to *mine our day for the jewels* that we might have missed in the day's unfolding. The hope is that through developing the practice of paying attention at the end of each day to God's presence and purposes, we might actually, at some point, be able to *recognize* and be attentive to Him as the events are happening.

Questions

What keeps you from being able to *recognize*?
What helps?
How is the word *recognize* relevant in your life right now?
How will you begin to pay attention to God in your life?

Chapter Two

Release

re-lease [ri-lees]: to free from anything that restrains; to free from confinement, bondage, obligation, pain; to let go; to give up, relinquish, or surrender (a right, claim, etc.).

Let us throw off everything that hinders and the sin that so easily entangles. (Hebrews 12:1)

Have this attitude in yourselves which was also in Christ Jesus, who, although He existed in the form of God, did not regard equality with God a thing to be grasped, but emptied Himself.... (Philippians 2:5-7)

As strange as it may seem, my career path has tended to run in decades (or almost anyway): nine years on staff with Young Life, ten years working in a local church, nine more years with Young Life, and now two years (and counting) working in the area of spiritual formation with Core Leadership. Looking back, this journey has been both incredibly interesting and extraordinarily beautiful. Each transition—each leaving and each new beginning—has been so very unique, both in the ways in which the transition came about, and how God led and guided along the way. And each has deposited something extremely valuable of God's heart into my soul; something that could be formed within me in no other way.

One of the stops in this amazing journey involved the ten years I spent working in a wonderful church in a suburban area of one of the most beautiful cities I've ever been in. Okay, okay, I have to admit, it was actually my hometown... and the church I grew up in. Well, I say the church I grew up in, but it is actually the church I started going to after coming to faith my senior year in high school. It is a community that, through the years, has invested so much in me, both in growing my faith and supporting God's call on my life; as well as praying faithfully for my family and our ministry along the way. Which made it all the sweeter when they called and asked if I might *come home* and invest in the lives of students and families in my hometown.

The ten years I spent there were some of the richest, most formative years of my entire spiritual journey; a time when God drew me to himself with an intimacy and intensity I had not yet known or experienced. It was during those years that my first book, the Blue Book (a spiritual journal/devotional of sorts), came into being. It was a time and a space that produced fertile soil in my soul, for which I am eternally grateful. So much of who I am now in Christ was formed during those ten years.

My primary task at the church was to help create volunteer teams of adults that felt called to invest daily in the lives of students (middle school through college). My job was to pray for, care for, and invest in them—and serve alongside them—as they invested in the lives of kids. And, over the next seven to nine years, God provided. He called the most loving, passionate, faithful group of volunteers that I could've ever imagined. He provided so many gifted folks that it made my job easy. And the relationships that came out of that time are still some of the ones that I hold most dear.

About nine years into this adventure I began to sense a restlessness growing within me. And I began to wonder if this restlessness was coming from God, or simply from me. So I began to try and pay attention to it, and to God, and see what might be at its core. "After all," I figured, "maybe this is just a season I am going through that will come and go in a short period of time." But it didn't go away, it actually continued to grow; which didn't mean it was definitely from God, but did mean that was a good possibility.

Most often, in my life thus far, when God is really trying to get my attention he will use repetition. Knowing me the way he does, I guess he knows that I can be a little slow on the uptake sometimes and that he needs to say something several different times, and in several different ways, before I recognize that he is actually speaking. That was definitely the case in this particular instance. I began to notice the same theme, or word, coming from several different directions. A scripture about him *doing something new* (Isaiah 43:18-19). *"Forget the former things; do not dwell on the past. See, I am doing a new thing! Now it springs up; do you not perceive it?"* And then a song about *"wondering where the winds were trying to take me, overnight, if I never did resist."* (David Wilcox, *Slipping Through My Fist*) A book about letting go, unclenching our fists, and opening our hands in surrender to God's agenda and direction. (*With Open Hands* by Henri Nouwen) Plus several conversations with dear and trusted friends who helped put words to things they didn't even know were going on within me.

As the process went on, I was becoming more and more convinced that it was, indeed, God speaking. And what he was saying was confirming what had already been growing in my heart for some time. He was asking me to let go of this life I'd grown comfortable with over the past nine years and step out into the new and unknown. The problem was, although I knew he was telling me to leave, I did not yet know where he was telling me to go. So I sat in that tension for a few weeks and prayed.

"Surely God would tell me where I am going before he asks me to step away from where I am, right?" All you have to do is look at the pages of scripture to know that God doesn't usually operate that way. In fact, it usually seems to be just the opposite; almost as if he is saying, "How can you take hold of what's next if your hands are still full of what was, or is? You must let go, because release comes before receive." And at that point I was certain I was hearing him clearly: "You must let go of where you are, before I will tell you where we are going. You must let go of one trapeze bar, and completely trust me in the *in between* (the "liminal space," as Richard Rohr calls it) before the new bar will appear." Because it is in this *in between* — where we are so vulnerable and receptive — that God does some of his very best work.

So I let go. I told my dear friends at the church that I was leaving and trying to follow the Spirit of God to a yet-to-be-determined destination. Don't think me terribly heroic — or stupid for that matter — for, as we talked, it seemed like the wisest course of action would be for me to leave at the end of the school year, which would allow the church time to find a replacement and give me a period of time to discern what God's next steps might be for me and my family.

Thus, I embarked on a seven or eight month-long process of listening to God and seeking his direction for my life and ministry. And, of course, during that time I uncovered many other areas where I simply needed to open my hands and let go: all of my plans, and schemes, and agendas, and hopes; as well as all of my fears, and doubts, and my need for control. Thus, it turned into an entire season of *release*.

Release is such a huge part of the spiritual journey, probably because of our tendency to hold on to things. In our heart of hearts we are all hoarders by nature. Our lives and our hearts are just so full. And when I say full in this context, I don't mean full in a good way. I don't mean full in the way Jesus talked about in John 10:10 when he said, "I have come that they may have life and have it to the full." I mean full in the sense that we are so full of our own stuff—full of ourselves, if you will—that there is no room for God to do a work within us.

We are full of regret and shame and guilt. We are full of secrets and lies and sin. We are full of worry and anxiety and fear. We are full of insecurity and inadequacy and need. And we are full of our own attitudes and plans and agendas. As a result of all of this, we fill our lives, and thus our schedules, with things to do, and places to go, and people to see. We live lives trying (clinging and grasping) desperately to prove our worth and make a name for ourselves.

We are simply *full*. And when we are full, particularly of those types of things, there is no room for anything else. The simple fact is that if your hands are full, you can't hold anything else. It is the same with our hearts and souls. If they are packed full of our own stuff, then there is no room within us for God to move and to work. That's why there is a constant need for release; an opening and an emptying. The practice of release creates space within us for God.

To finish the story, after about seven months of praying and seeking and pushing on closed doors, God finally made our next destination clear. And it was not at all in the direction I thought it would be, nor was it to a place or a job I thought he would be leading us to at that point in our lives (surprise! surprise!). But it was to the perfect place and the perfect job for the next stage of the journey. At the age of 42, I went back into youth ministry through Young Life, and it was the perfect place for what he most wanted to do in and through me and my family for the next season of our lives. All because he had given me the courage and the grace to open my tightly clenched fists, trust his heart, and receive the gift he had for us.

Clenched Fists and Open Hands

In the book I mentioned earlier, *With Open Hands*, Henri Nouwen relates a story that provides a powerful image. An old woman in a mental health facility has a small coin in her hands she is absolutely terrified someone will try to take away from her. Because of that fear, her fists are clenched so tightly around the coin that the circulation in her fingers is almost completely cut off. In fact, she holds on so tightly to it that no one can possibly pry her fingers open to see what it is that she is so terrified to let go of. Controlled by her fear, she hangs on for dear life, as if the coin were more valuable to her than all the treasures of the earth combined.

That is how we often live our lives, with clenched fists. We hang on to old patterns, old worries, old sources of value and worth, old ways of seeing and being, because we are afraid that if they are taken away from us, we will be left with nothing. The problem is that nothing can be received from God until we are willing to let go of our clenched-fisted approach to life, and to relationships—particularly our relationship with Him — and open our hands to whatever He desires to give us, or to make us into.

Clenched fists represent a refusal, a resistance, an unwillingness to trust. They are all about possessiveness and demand and entitlement; all of which are absolutely lethal to our spiritual lives. They involve clinging tightly to our own stuff, or our own agenda, or our own reputation — even our own hurts and wounds. When our hands are so tightly wrapped around our own *stuff*, it squeezes the life right out of our soul; which was created to be filled by God and God alone. Therefore clenched fists distance us from the intimacy God desires both for us and with us. The bottom line is that clenched fists say *no* to God.

In order to be truly transformed, repentance — a change of mind, heart, and direction — must come about. We must move from clenched fists to open hands. Open hands say *yes* to God. They abandon agenda, control, and demand. They show a willingness and a desire to receive Him, and all the gifts of life along with him. A truly open hand holds absolutely nothing. It simply lies open, waiting to receive whatever God chooses to give.

Purgation

The word the saints use to convey this idea of release is *purgation*, which feels a little more intense than the word release, and carries with it a slightly different picture. Purgation is defined as *the act or state of being purged; purification.* The word comes from the Latin word *purgatio* which means "to cleanse," which comes from the root *purus*, meaning pure. Thus purgation describes the process by which we — by his grace and power — attempt to empty ourselves of all that is not God, so that in turn we may be pure and open and ready to be filled to overflowing with his Spirit, his life and his power. It is the creation of sacred space within us for God to inhabit; which for the saints was the first movement in a three-part dance of purgation, illumination, and union. Therefore, purgation does not involve becoming empty simply for empty's sake, but becoming empty in order to be filled.

As part of this emptying process, we have to come to terms with the sin that fills a significant amount of our inner space. When we hold on to sinful patterns, attitudes, and behavior, how can we ever expect that there would be any fruitful space in our hearts and souls for God to move and to work and to dwell? If we want to live the lives we most deeply long for, and the lives God most deeply longs to live in us, we simply must let go of our sin, open our hands to God, and give Him total ownership of every area of our lives.

Confession

The practice of confession is one way to do that. Confession allows us to come face-to-face with our sin: to name it, own it, and admit it to God, and, in some cases, to a trusted spiritual friend. Then confession allows us to let go of our sin and give it fully to God, creating space within us for him to dwell. Confession unblocks the inner wells of the life of God's Spirit within us. It allows us a type of emptying, a letting go, a freedom from an immense burden.

Through the practice of confession we are able to let go not only of our sin, but also of the guilt and shame and remorse we drag along behind us as we journey through life. It reminds me of a powerful scene in the movie *The Mission* where one of the main characters, Rodrigo Mendoza (played by Robert De Niro), due to his enormous guilt and shame over dreadful things he has done in his life, imposes a penance upon himself of carrying a heavy bag of armor to the top of a high mountain. The journey is grueling and treacherous, and incredibly painful to watch, as he struggles and fights his way to the top of the mountain. It is not until he reaches the top that the ropes are cut and the bag is tossed into the depths of the sea. At this, he dissolves in a pool of tears: tears of relief, tears of freedom, tears of release.

We tend to live our lives in much the same way, dragging our baggage behind us wherever we go, just like Rodrigo Mendoza. But because of the work of Christ, there is no need for us to do that, we can release it all right now. All of our guilt, and all of our shame, and all of our remorse and regret can be cut loose and tossed into the sea of his great mercy and love.

The practice of confession allows us to do just that, relying on God's promise that, for those who love and trust him, he has separated our sins as far from us as the east is from the west. If you'll notice, he doesn't say as far as the north is from the south. Why is that? It is because, although very far apart, north and south eventually meet (at the poles). As you travel north on the globe, when you get to the North Pole, you then begin traveling south. East and west however, never meet. If you travel east on the globe you will be eternally traveling east, or if you travel west, eternally traveling west — the two never meet. So it is with our forgiveness in Christ. When we truly release our sin to him and receive his forgiveness, we are completely captured by his love...and, through confession, finally we are set free!

A Beautiful Example

I'm not sure how often it happens, but in 2013, Ash Wednesday and Valentine's Day were back-to-back. It caught me more than a little bit off guard. I mean, there you are on Wednesday having ashes placed upon your forehead and reading scripture (Joel 2:12-14) that invites you *to return to* the Lord *with all our heart, with fasting and weeping and mourning,* and *to rend your heart and not your garments.* Those are verses that know both the value and the necessity of release and repentance in the spiritual journey. Ash Wednesday is a day filled with heaviness and sadness, mourning and sorrow, weeping and contrition, darkness and desperation.

And then, the very next day, it's Valentine's Day, and you are sitting across the table from the one you love and adore, in an incredibly romantic restaurant, filled to overflowing with *affection* as you celebrate the life and the love that you are so privileged to share with each other. Valentine's

Day is a day when our hearts and our focus are on love and affection, romance and delight, laughter and joy. A bit of a contrast, wouldn't you say? To be filled with *sorrow* one day and filled with *affection* the next; a pretty odd pairing to say the least, or so it would seem. But maybe it's not so odd after all.

In fact, there's a beautiful story in Luke that brings these strange bedfellows together and gives us a picture of the process we are talking about: the marriage of release and receive. The process of recognizing the depth of our sin, releasing it to God, receiving His unconditional forgiveness, and, as a result, being completely captured and overwhelmed by His great love.

It is the story of a woman (Luke 7:36-50) who comes to Jesus while he is dining in the home of a man known as Simon the Pharisee. She is not named, but everyone seems to know who she is. In fact, she has quite a reputation in town. And it would seem that her reputation is so well known that it has actually become her identity; that is, until she meets Jesus.

We are not told exactly when or how that meeting happened, but somewhere along the way these two had encountered each other and it had marked her forever, completely changing everything about her. In Luke 7, here she was, on this particular evening, entering a house that she had no business entering — the house of a Pharisee. She shouldn't have been there at all, I mean a woman "like her" just didn't barge into the house of a Pharisee, especially when he was entertaining guests.

But this particular Pharisee had invited Jesus to dine with him—as well as a bunch of his Pharisee buddies I'm sure—so they could all get an up close look at this man that everyone was talking about. Whether it was curiosity or hostility that inspired the invitation we are not sure; although we can probably guess. All we are sure of is that he had invited Jesus into his house, and Jesus, and his other guests were reclining at the table.

It is in the midst of this dinner party that *she* came; uninvited and uncaring that she was uninvited. She didn't care about protocol. She didn't care about political correctness. She didn't care what anyone thought or said. All she cared about was getting to the feet of her beloved Jesus. She only had eyes for him, so she entered the room and didn't look back, making a beeline straight for his feet.

And when she got there, just look at what happened: *she stood behind him at his feet weeping, and began to wet his feet with her tears. Then she wiped them with her hair, kissed them and poured perfume on them (Luke 7:38).* Did you catch that? She was *weeping* and she was *kissing*; sorrow and affection, Ash Wednesday and Valentine's Day. Two things that are seemingly contrary, but are actually inseparable. It is the gospel brought to life. These two things must always be connected in the life of faith. For the gospel is more than just one or the other, it is always both.

There must always be a *weeping*; it is a necessary part of the picture. Weeping involves a deep recognition of our utter sinfulness, brokenness, helplessness, and desperation. It is what happens within us when we come face-to-face with the absolute horror of our sin—the very sin that crucified Christ. And this *weeping* is much more than simply crying, it is much deeper than that. It is an activity that, although terribly difficult, is also deeply redemptive because it can make space within us for God's love and his healing to enter in. The tears of this woman were not normal tears, they came from somewhere deep within her, from that place of godly sorrow that Paul talks about in 2 Corinthians 7:10. It is the type of godly sorrow that leads to confession, and to repentance.

But as necessary as the *weeping* is, we can't stop there. There is so much more. We don't release just to release. We release in order to receive. That's where the *kissing* comes in; for not only did she *weep*, but she also *kissed*. As a matter of fact the literal translation of the Greek is that she *kissed* (his feet) *much*. She smothered him with kisses. She could not stop. She just went on and on.

Just look at verse 45: *this woman, from the time I entered, has not stopped kissing my feet.* His love for her had completely captured her heart. It had kindled an uncontrollable affection deep within her that simply could not be contained. She could not stop if she wanted to, so smitten with love for Him was she. Her empty heart had been invaded and inhabited by an Extravagant Love. And from now on, everything about her would be different.

Releasing the False Self

And before we leave the topic of release, it is important that we not stop too near the surface, but keep pressing on and digging down until we have a true and accurate idea of exactly what it is that we need to let go of. It is easy enough to spot the things nearest the surface and say, "I need to let go of impatience, or frustration, or anger." Or "I need to release my fear, or anxiety, or insecurity." But these are just the outward signs of a much deeper work to be done. What lies beneath these things is the real issue.

At our core, we all carry around images of God, and, in turn, images of ourselves, that are simply not accurate. I'm not talking about what we say we believe about God and about ourselves, I'm talking about how the way we live our lives shows us what we really believe. What we really believe about God, and what we really believe about ourselves, comes out most clearly in the way we live. If I am filled with anxiety and consumed by worry, what does that say about what I really believe about God? And what does it say about what I really believe about myself? Does it say that at my core I really believe that God is either not big enough to take care of me, or that he doesn't really want to? And does that make me believe that I am on my own and better become self-sufficient because I am not worth God really loving or taking care of? These are the kinds of hidden beliefs that I am talking about. Our patterns and our behavior give us the best clues about what we really believe.

One of the biggest battles in my life and heart is my sense of insecurity. If I let it, it will dominate every relationship, circumstance, and activity in my life. To be honest, sometimes it feels like a bottomless pit within me, and that I am a massive black hole of need. Where in the world does all of that come from? What lies underneath my constant fear and insecurity? As always, when I turn to scripture it can give me a pretty good clue.

Isaiah 62 is one of my favorite chapters in all of scripture. Why? Because in it God's people have forgotten; they have forgotten both who God is and who they are to him. They have been taken into captivity and have been there so long that they have started listening to the voices of their captors, and have actually started to believe that what their captors are saying about them, and about their God, is true. Their enemies are constantly calling them names, and over time they have begun to believe that these names describe who they really are. They have forgotten who God is and who they were created to be. Instead of believing that they are the *Children of God*, they have begun to believe that they are really *Desolate* and *Deserted*. In Isaiah 62 God has had enough, and He comes to his people to remind them of who they are — their true name and their true identity.

I find that it is the same with each of us. I firmly believe that *all of us live out of the name we most believe to be true about us.* For Israel it was Desolate and Deserted, not worth God's care, not worthy of his attention or presence. For me, the name I live by most of the time is *Not Enough*. Somewhere along the course of my life I have become convinced — by voices or events or painful memories — that I am worthless and no good, that I can't do anything well and have no value. And when I live out of that name, it has a really ugly effect on my life. Whenever I am faced with a situation in which I am unable to do whatever it is I'm *supposed* to be able to do, it is like a toxic poison is released within me and begins to spew out upon whoever might be standing in its path at the moment.

One of the times when this becomes most evident is when I am trying to build, assemble, or repair something. I don't know why, but I am mechanically challenged. For some reason my mind, and thus my hands, just don't work on that wavelength. I am a DIY nightmare; or should I say DIY is my worst nightmare. When my wife Carol and I were first married and moved into our first apartment, she assumed that I would naturally and easily be able to do the things so many other guys do so naturally and easily. She couldn't have been more wrong and she was, unfortunately, in for a rude awakening in finding this out. Whenever I tried to hang something, assemble something, or repair something, in about 99% of the cases whatever I was attempting to do ended up much worse at the end of the process than it was at the beginning. And when this would happen, a sense of intense rage and anger would rise up within me and pour forth from me, which made us both stop and ask, "Where in the world did that come from?" It was telling that the rage was never directed at her, but was always directed at myself.

The rage was coming from what I had feared to be true all of my life. It was coming from that false name that I lived by; the one I had come to believe was really true — who I really was — much to my dismay. And this particular circumstance simply ignited it, like gasoline on a fire. Somewhere, somehow, I desperately needed to identify that false name, call it out for the lie that it was, and let it go. But this is more easily said than done.

It actually took years of prayer and reflection and conversation to recognize what was really going on; then name it and begin the process of releasing it. A few years ago, by God's grace and power, I was finally able to come to the point where I said, "I have believed my name is *Not Enough*, but that is not who I am, that is not my true name. It is a lie from the pit of hell and I refuse to live by it anymore." Once I recognized that name for the lie that it was, then I could begin the process of releasing it. And only after I released it could I receive my new name from God, the one he knew me by and longed for me to live out of. It is who I really am, the name God called me by when he breathed me into being. We will talk more about that in the next chapter.

What about you? Is there a name that comes to mind? Is there something that comes up from deep within you that tells you lies that the enemy would love for you to believe? Maybe it is something you were actually called at some point in your life (whoever made up the saying that sticks and stones will break your bones but names will never hurt you couldn't have been more wrong), or maybe you came up with it on your own in response to some of the broken, hurtful places of your life. Regardless of where it came from, its roots go deep, and the process of discovering and releasing this false name can take a long time. But if you want genuine transformation to occur, it is a necessity.

Practice

Buy two of those stick-on name tags that say "Hello, my name is" at the top. Sit in silence before the Lord. Try to simply be present with him and allow him to be present with you. When you have come to some sense of stillness, look at the name tags and ask God to reveal to you the names you have lived by to this point in your life. Is there one that stands out? Write it down on the name tag. Ask God to reveal to you how living out of that name has affected your life, and how that name still impacts your life today. Now, take the name tag and tear it to little pieces, releasing that old, false identity to him. Listen deeply as he tells you, "That is not your name." Hold on to the second name tag, we'll use it after the next chapter.

Questions

Where in are you living with clenched fists?
What would it look like to open your hands?
Where does the word release seem most relevant right now?
What do you need to release to God?

Chapter Three

Receive

re·ceive [ri-seev]: to take into one's possession; to have (something) bestowed, conferred, etc.; to have delivered (something) or brought to one.

*He came to that which was his own, but his own did not **receive** him. [12] Yet to all who did **receive** him, to those who believed in his name, he gave the right to become children of God — [13] children born not of natural descent, nor of human decision or a husband's will, but born of God. (John 1:11-13)*

For the past ten years I have been the chaplain of our local high school football team. It is something that has been an absolute joy and delight for me; I can only hope it has been half as good for the players and coaches. This group of people has made such an impact on my heart and soul through the years that there is no way I can possibly repay them. I am just so grateful they have given me the privilege of being able to hang around.

One of my friends is named Jonathan. Jonathan is one of the best kids I have ever met, and a heck of a football player. Everything just seems to come so naturally for him. On top of being kind and respectful and humble and hardworking and engaging, he is an amazing athlete who was invaluable as a player and a leader for all four of the years he wore the black and orange. An all-state defensive back and the school career leader in interceptions, he also returned punts and kickoffs. Watching him on returns, and talking with him about it, taught me something incredibly valuable about my spiritual journey. Watching Jonathan return kicks gave me one of the best pictures I can imagine of what it looks like to *receive*.

I mean, it's such an abstract concept, particularly when you're talking about receiving something from God. What does it even look like to *receive* something from God? And what am I supposed to do? What is important to remember and keep in mind? All great — and relevant — questions, but questions we have a hard time answering. Well, never fear, just sit back and allow Jonathan to teach us what *receiving* is all about.

First, notice that receiving requires a certain posture. As
we said in the last chapter, it requires empty and open
hands, ready to lay hold of *it,* whenever *it* comes and
whatever *it* might be. It is a posture of expectation; the
returner knows the ball is coming, there is no doubt in his
mind, he just has to be ready for the how and the where and
the when. This posture of expectation requires us to believe
something. It requires us to fully believe that God is always
working, always moving, always speaking; that there is
always something for us to receive. It is up to us to
recognize where or how or when, and to open our hands to
receive whatever it is that he's giving us. For if we do not
believe that he is going to give to us, then we will not be
ready when *it* comes. We are likely to be distracted or to be
lulled to sleep, and miss *it* altogether.

Which brings us to another characteristic I've noticed of a
receptive posture: attentiveness. If you know for a fact that
the ball is indeed coming, then you must be ready and
attentive and alert for however and wherever it might arrive.
We talked a good bit about this in the first chapter; the
significant role of attentiveness in the spiritual life. It is
quite possible that God, even this very day, has come, and
tried to get my attention. Perhaps he had something
precious of himself that he wanted to give to me, but I
simply wasn't paying attention. After all, God often comes
in ways and in forms that we do not expect or are not
looking for—see, for example, the story of the nativity in
Luke 1-2, as well as a plethora of other passages.

In fact, we cannot control how or where or when he will come; that's where waiting comes in. A kick returner cannot become good at receiving kicks without learning how to *wait*. And apparently we cannot be good at receiving the things God desires to give us without learning to do the same. Waiting is so essential to the receiving process. It is also essential to the life of the Spirit within us. The scriptures bear witness to this; they are absolutely full of places where we are simply called to *wait on the Lord*. That is where we so often fail for we are impatient people. We want to be in control, so we try to take matters into our own hands and *make something happen;* which generally does more harm than good. It's like a kick returner growing so impatient that he runs and grabs the ball off the tee before it has ever been kicked. But the painful truth is that we cannot force the action; we cannot control — as much as we'd like to — the when, where, or how of this process. It is the kicker that must initiate the kickoff, just as it is the Creator who must initiate our re-creation (or transformation). Our role is simply to wait.

But what happens *after* the ball has been kicked and you see it in the air? That is the most important part of the receiving process. That is where we must *take hold of whatever we have received and make it our own*. Technically, in a football game, the ball does not belong to the offense until they take possession of the ball. Therefore, once we recognize that God is at work or is present, and has something for us to receive, we must get our hands on it, *take hold of it, and make it our own*. We must make it a part of us.

Without the taking hold, we have never really *received* what was there to be given to us in the first place; the ball is not yet ours, it is still lying on the ground.

So what does the word *receive* look like in a spiritual context? It looks like fully believing that God is always up to something, waiting in eager expectation for whatever that "something" may be. It looks like being awake and alert and attentive to how or where he might come to us and, once we see him, receive what he has for us, take hold of it and make it our own. And who knows, if we diligently practice the art of receiving maybe it will become as natural for us as it is for my friend Jonathan.

Bestow

One of my new favorite words of the spiritual life is the word *bestow*. And I don't mean new in the sense that it just arrived on the scene, but new in the sense that it is brand new to me. I suppose it has been there all along, lying on the page, waiting for me to dig a little and uncover the treasure it holds, but for some reason I have simply passed over it all these years. Then one day I stumbled upon it — and we all know that it wasn't stumbling at all, but God's hand and His leading — and was completely captured by its beauty. For the word *bestow* is indeed a magnificent treasure. And I think the reason I have been so captured by it recently is because of the very thing we are talking about.

You see, *bestow* is not something that can be achieved or accomplished or even earned; by its very nature it is something that can only be given or conferred. It is a gift, something we can never hope to attain on our own, but something that can only be done for us, or to us. *Bestow* focuses all of the attention on the heart of the Giver, and not on the worthiness, or skill, or aptitude of the receiver. It has everything to do with God, and the intricate care with which he made us, and the extravagant love with which he loves us. *Bestow* is all about receiving.

This is especially true when it comes to our identity. A few months ago, as I was meditating on this treasure, I came to a realization. I tend to go through life trying— in futility, I might add—to *create* a self each day rather than to simply *receive* a self each day. And any self that is created by anything or anyone other the Creator, the God that breathed me into being, can only be false. Any *self* that I create or manufacture is a false self because it is just a cheap imitation, adaptation, or distortion of the *me* I was created to be by the One who dreamt me into being before the foundations of the earth.

My true identity can only be *bestowed*, it can never be achieved. So my challenge, each and every day, is to stop the ongoing pattern of trying, in desperation, to create a self that has in fact already been *fearfully and wonderfully made;* and to simply receive my true self in peace and in freedom from the God who made me uniquely and loves me dearly. It is funny how much I strive to make a name for myself, when only he can give me the name I was made to bear—my true name.

How incredibly freeing! It is as if God is saying: *"I have given you your value and your worth. I have bestowed it upon you and it can never be lost. So stop measuring. Stop earning. Stop comparing. Stop performing. Your worth is not hanging in the balance. It does not depend on anything you achieve, or on any accomplishment you attain. So relax. Live in the freedom of knowing you are loved deeply and fully and completely – as well as eternally. Instead of working so hard to prove yourself, just fall in love with Me."*

Receiving Our True Name

You will be called by a new name that the mouth of the Lord will bestow. (Isaiah 62:2)

Israel had forgotten her name (Isaiah 62), forgotten who she truly was, so God comes to her. It is almost as if he could not stay away. His heart would not allow him to be silent any longer, so he speaks to his people and reminds them of who they are and calls them by their true name.

"Your name is not Desolate, the name of your land is not Deserted. You are not worthless and unloved, you are mine. You are My Delight and have immeasurable value to me. You are like a crown of splendor in my hand, something worthy of adorning the head of the King of Kings. I look at you with a heart more full of love than you will ever know. In fact, I look at you with more love and desire than that of a bridegroom as he looks at his new bride coming down the aisle. You are so beautiful to me, and I love you more than you could hope for in your wildest dreams. You mean so much to me that I have a special name picked out for you; one

that I will give you when we are together forever in Paradise. But for now, know that I call you Holy People, Redeemed of the Lord. I call you Sought After."

And so it is for each of us. Our world has made us forget who we really are and has made us believe we are something far less than we were intended to be. Therefore, God comes to us and speaks, and reminds us of our true value, our true identity. We must be very careful to listen to his voice, for he is offering us an incredible gift; one that we must take hold of and make our own; one that we must receive. It is the gift of a new name.

Isn't that amazing! The God of all creation has a name that he has picked out especially for you. God has a pet name for you. And when he whispers it in your ear, it will make your soul stand on tiptoe as never before. It will cause your insides — and most likely your outsides too — to leap for joy in a way that you never have before. When you hear that name it will cause a "Yes!" to well up from deep within you. So, by all means, wait in eager expectation, pay careful attention, watch and listen attentively, and receive the incredible name God bestows on each of his children.

Mine

When he was in high school, my oldest son Tim ran track and cross country, which meant, of course, that my wife and I had to become experts in the art of watching track and cross country meets. Now there's no real skill needed to watch a track meet, the parameters are kind of set for you —

it's mostly about timing. But there is definitely an art to watching a cross country meet: Where will I watch from? How will get to I see the biggest part of the race? How can I best encourage without embarrassing or humiliating my child (a great question for every parent to ask themselves)? And then, how will I get to a good place to see the finish?

One thing that is great about cross country meets is that there are no bleachers, you are right there with the runners, right in the middle of the action. And, surprisingly, there is plenty of action if you are paying attention.

For instance, there are all kinds of people at these meets. There are the meet officials who check everyone in and make sure everyone has a number, knows the course, and understands the rules. The officials uphold the rules and make sure everyone operates by them. Break the rules and the runner must pay the consequences.

There are also coaches. Coaches come in all shapes and sizes, with all kinds of different styles. Some coaches are screamers; from start to finish they yell words that are at times encouraging and at other times not so encouraging to their runners. Then there are coaches who are measurers; keeping track of times and splits and seeing how the performance of each runner measures up to both their potential, as well as their past performances. Then there are coaches who are instructors and teachers. These coaches are not as worried about the end result as they are concerned about whether each runner is doing it "the right way."

And of course, there are parents. Some parents are so involved you would think they were running the race themselves. And others are so uninvolved that they stay in the car, or read a book, or talk on the phone, waiting for the whole thing to be over.

I recall one particular race toward the end of the season — one that would determine which runners would advance to the state meet. I was standing next to a woman near the finish line as the girls' race was finishing. There was a group of about twelve girls sprinting toward the finish line with only ten spots available for the state meet. They were giving it everything they had. And as they got within about fifty feet of the finish line, it became apparent that two of them were not going to make that top ten. It also became apparent that the woman I was standing beside was the mother of one of the two.

I'll never forget, that as this girl passed the spot where her mother was standing, her mother yelled at her, "Maureen! Can't you do any better than that?" And you could see on the young girl's face that the words of her mother had wounded her much more deeply than any race ever could or would. To be honest, I wanted to turn and punch the lady's lights out. But of course I didn't. I did, however, let that memory live on in my heart and my mind as a great example of something I never want to do or to be. Yes, there are all different types of parents.

And then there's me, just a dad. I know all of the runners on our team and I want them all to do well, but if I'm honest, as I'm standing out on that race course, I'm looking for one runner in particular. I'm looking for mine. It is impossible to put into words, for something happens deep in the heart of a father when he sees the one who is his. The minute I spot him, my heart skips a beat and before I know it, there is a smile on my face. It has nothing to do with where he is finishing or how well he is running. It's simply the fact that he's mine. The next thing I know I'm standing on tiptoe, and then I'm hopping up and down; so glad, so proud, so filled with love and affection.

I don't think that most of us realize that God feels the very same way (and then some) about us. Some of us might imagine God as a race official, just waiting for us to mess up or take a short cut so he can disqualify us from the race. Others might imagine God as a coach, constantly measuring and grading our performance and, if we don't measure up, we're taken out of the race. Still others might imagine God as an overbearing parent who rolls his eyes and yells as we're trying our hardest, "Can't you do any better than that?"

But the truth is that God is really like a Dad. He is a father, whose heart skips a beat when he sees us because he is so filled with love and affection for us. He is an *Abba* (as Jesus called him) who loves us so much that we bring a smile to his face and joy to his heart, simply because we are his.

There was a woman in the gospels (Mark 5:24-34) who found this out for herself. We are not told her name, which is perhaps symbolic of how she felt about herself. At the very best she was just a face in the crowd, a nobody. But it was far worse than that, because she had been bleeding inside for twelve years. I'm sure dealing with the physical effects of the disease was bad enough, but the social and emotion damage associated with it was even worse. For twelve years she had been called *unclean*. Can you imagine having to live by that name for twelve years? She was not just *a nobody*; she was a reject, an outcast, someone to be avoided at all costs.

And so she comes up behind Jesus in a crowd, thinking if she can just touch the edge of his robe, that would be enough to heal her. And when she reaches for him and touches his robe, she is immediately healed. But that's not the best part of the story. The best part of the story is what he says to her: "Daughter, your faith has healed you. Go in peace and be freed from your suffering."

Did you see that? He calls her daughter. Almost as if to say, *"My dear one, you are not unclean. You are not a reject. You are not an outcast. That is not your name. You are mine! You are my daughter! Let that be the thing that gives you the worth and the value, the healing and the wholeness you most deeply long for. Let go of Unclean and receive Mine."*

Practice

Find a quiet place where you can spend some time in uninterrupted silence. After you spend a few minutes coming to stillness, turn to Isaiah 62 and read the chapter. Read it slowly, listening for God's voice to you in his Word. Pay careful attention to anything that might resonate within you for some reason. Read it like you are digging for the treasure hidden in the field. When something strikes a chord within you, stop and listen to what God might want to say to you. Notice the names. Which ones resonate with you? Now take the other name tag and ask God to give you his name for you. What name do you long to be called at the core of your being? Write that name on the name tag. Listen to him speak that name to you. Listen to him say it over and over again. Become convinced that it is what is really true about you. Put that name tag in a place where you will see it and cherish it often — maybe in your journal. Now tell him what he means to you. Spend the last few minutes just being with him and enjoying his presence.

Questions

What are you most deeply longing to receive from God?
What helps you be more receptive to him?
What is your biggest obstacle to receiving from him?
How is the word *receive* relevant to you right now?

Chapter Four

Believe

be ·lieve [bih-leev]: to have confidence in the truth, the existence, or the reliability of something; to have a conviction that a person (or thing) is.

*He came to that which was his own, but his own did not receive him. [12] Yet to all who did receive him, to those who **believed** in his name, he gave the right to become children of God — [13] children born not of natural descent, nor of human decision or a husband's will, but born of God. (John 1:11-13)*

My wife has worked in the fitness industry for the better part of the last twenty years. She absolutely loves exercise and nutrition, and all that comes along with helping people live healthy lives. Given that fact, it's a wonder she married, and puts up with, a guy like me. The only future I have in the fitness industry is being the person for the "before" picture in the ads and commercials. Be that as it may, given her line of work, one of the things she likes to do — and I'll have to admit that I enjoy it as well — is to watch weight loss reality shows. I can readily see the appeal for her, but, as far as I'm concerned, I guess I'd rather watch people exercising than actually have to do it myself. But seriously, the reason I like to watch these shows is because of the transformations that take place on them. The people and the stories are incredibly inspiring to watch.

On a typical show, a group of people who appear to be trapped in a dark and hopeless place in life, prisoners it would seem of their own destructive patterns and ways of thinking, are whisked away to a controlled, structured, and supportive environment where they are given the opportunity to reclaim their lives. And reclaim their lives they do! Over the course of the show — which can last from six months to a year depending on the format — we are able to join them and share in their remarkably transformational journey.

To help them along the way, participants are given personal trainers whose role is to provide wisdom, encouragement, and guidance in their journey. In each episode, participants learn a new set of life skills that will lead them toward a healthier lifestyle; a large emphasis is placed on losing weight and how much weight is lost each week. But the contestants, and the trainers, know that there is a bigger story lying underneath their need to lose weight. There is the story of how they got to where they are and what life experiences contributed to them living out of that dysfunctional place.

These contestants each have certain issues and wounds and broken places in their lives that have made them believe specific things about themselves and about their world. This is where it gets really interesting. The trainers know that they can help them lose weight, but unless they change their beliefs, then all the changes these folks make in "the house" are only cosmetic and temporary.

Belief is such a huge factor in the process of transformation. That's why the word is used so often in the scriptures — particularly in the gospel of John. John knew that until there was a significant change of heart and mind, there would never be a significant change in behavior. Belief, to him, was not something that could be separated from life. Unfortunately that doesn't appear to be the case in our current culture. Through the years, we have cheapened the word *belief* to the point where we can say we believe something, yet it has absolutely no impact on the way we live our lives. Merely acknowledging something verbally, however, is not belief at all. True belief goes much deeper than that.

Years ago I was leading a retreat for some of the high school and middle school students at our church. It was a big undertaking and I recruited lots of quality folks to help make sure it was the best week it could possibly be. One of those was Bob, a man who had had a significant impact on my life when I was a high school and college student, and was still a mentor to me. Bob's job at camp was to run the "work crew," which was the group of students and adults who were assigned to do the work necessary for the camp to function, so that the kids that came on the retreat could just be there and focus on listening to what God was saying to them. Bob also had the task of investing in the spiritual lives of the folks who were "working" while they were at camp.

A couple of days into the experience I asked Bob how it was going. He said that the work was getting done, but the spiritual conversation and growth of the folks on the work crew was coming a little slower. "Every time I try to talk with them about life and faith," he said, "I find that all the good words have already been used up. They simply don't mean anything to them anymore. I'm trying to speak a whole new vocabulary and trying to reclaim the significance of some of these great words."

My fear is that many words — not just the word *belief* — have suffered the same fate. Somehow we need to reclaim these great words and recapture their significance and their power for a culture that has lost track of their real meaning. After all, what good will it do for us to *receive* a wonderful word from God if we never really *believe* it, if it never really becomes a part of us? It would be like the seed sown in one of the unfruitful soils — either hard, rocky, or thorny — holding enormous possibility, but in the end coming to nothing. If what we *receive* from God is to have any genuine impact on us, if it is to come to life within us and become a part of us, it must be planted in good, fertile soil; the rich soil of *belief*. *Belief* is absolutely essential in the process of becoming.

Convinced

The Greek word for believe is *peitho*, which means to be *fully persuaded* of something. It is a central theme throughout all of scripture. Paul uses this word in Romans 8:38 when he talks about being absolutely *convinced* that nothing can ever separate us from the love of God in Christ Jesus. It is a word that has some substance to it, some rootedness, some resolve. It is a strong word; one that is able to withstand adverse conditions and circumstances. When we are absolutely convinced of something it goes all the way to the core of our being. When we are absolutely convinced of something we are not easily swayed or knocked off course. When we are absolutely convinced of something it always has an impact on our lives. But how does this *convincing* take place? How do we become absolutely convinced of something? How do we truly believe what we have received?

Listening

My kids are pretty much all grown up these days, but when they were younger, due to the nature of my job, I was out a lot at night. There were usually at least three, and sometimes four, nights a week when I was working and could not be home to help put them to bed. Looking back, I wish I would have had the wisdom in those days to realize how ridiculous that was, and that things would be just fine at "work" without me — but that's for another book. I guess I was too busy "climbing" to realize that there were other things that were much more important. Thank goodness I have a saint for a wife.

Anyway, I used to worry that, with not being around for their nightly routine during such a formative time, they might somehow forget the love and affection that I had for them. So when I would finally get home at night, I would go straight to their rooms. One at a time, I would cuddle up beside them in their beds, put my mouth right up to their ear, and begin to whisper whatever words of affection flowed from the deepest places of my heart.

Timothy, your Daddy loves you so much. I am so incredibly proud of you. You bring such deep joy to my heart. Michelle, you are my princess. I love and adore you so much and am so glad that God allowed me the gift of being your Dad. Hunter, you are such a delight to me and I love you more than you could ever imagine in your wildest dreams.

And so it would go. I would spend ten to fifteen minutes whispering in each of my kids' ears, because I wanted desperately for them to know the depths of my love for them. My hope was that if they heard it over and over again, even in their sleep, eventually they might come to believe it was true at the very core of their being. My hope was that by listening to my voice over and over again, they might become absolutely convinced. Obviously they needed to see it on a regular basis too, which I pray they did, but there is something very sweet and transforming about hearing that voice of love and affection consistently.

This is particularly true when we are talking about hearing the loving voice of the One who made us. If we are able to settle into some sort of silence and stop the clamoring of the false voices — both outside and within — that constantly barrage us with lies and half-truths and draw the ear of our hearts near to the mouth of God, then we might begin to hear the words of life, love, and affection that our hearts most deeply long to hear. And the more often we are still and silent and listening, the more often we will hear him speak. And the more often we hear him speak, the more likely the possibility that one day we will be convinced of what he's saying.

Hearing His Voice

One summer my daughter and I decided to watch the ESPYs — the ESPN annual awards show for excellence in sports. Now anyone who knows my daughter knows that she is a huge Peyton Manning fan; I think it has something to do with the fact that she got his autograph and a picture made with him when she was in first grade. Anyway, Peyton was scheduled to make an appearance on the ESPYs, so we sat down to watch.

For those who might have seen it, I'm sure you'll remember that Peyton was there to present Pat Summitt with the Arthur Ashe Courage Award. Peyton's words honoring her were filled to overflowing with kindness and respect and the utmost admiration — classic Peyton Manning. After his introduction, there was a video highlighting Coach Summitt's life, career, and achievements. It was absolutely beautiful! The video was filled with person after person telling their story of how Pat Summitt had impacted them, and how much she means to them, and what kind of amazing person she is. To top it all off, after the video Coach Summitt came forward with her son and humbly and gracefully accepted this prestigious award. It was incredibly powerful.

I sat there in awe of the whole thing, not really knowing what to say, not really able to move, and deeply, deeply affected by it all. In fact, after everyone had gone to bed that night, I went back and watched the whole thing again, wondering why it had impacted — and was continuing to impact — me so profoundly. Whatever it was doing in me would just not go away, so I continued to reflect on it.

Sitting in the dark, unable to sleep, I began to pray: "Lord, what is going on in me? What is it about this video that has affected me so deeply? What is this all about? What are you trying to say to me?" Not sensing any answer, and content with just wondering, I decided to go to bed. I got changed and laid down in the bed, still miles and miles from sleep.

And as my spirit calmed and my mind cleared, I heard that oh so familiar Voice whisper in the ear of my spirit,

"You desperately want people to feel that way about you." At this the tears began to roll down my cheeks because I knew it was the truth. It was not a voice of accusation; you know, the one you and I hear so often, the one that immediately turns us toward guilt and shame. Instead it was the Voice of One who loves me deeply and wants me to know the truth of my own heart.

And so I sat with (I guess technically I was lying down with) this recognition, or revelation, or whatever you might want to call it, grateful for the space and the silence to take in this truth and allow it to speak. Then, a few moments later, the Voice again whispered deeply into my heart and soul: *"I feel that way about you."* And then the tears came full-force as I was held in the intimately loving embrace of the One who knows me like no other and loves me more than I could ever ask or imagine. That night, that Voice, and those sweet words will mark me for a long, long time. It was the night when my Father, in his infinite tenderness, drew his mouth close to my ear and whispered his great affection to me.

The Desert

God actually speaks to us pretty regularly, if we will just create the space and make the time to hear him. It is all over the pages of scripture. That is why he is constantly calling people to the desert. And I don't mean desert in the sense of dry and lifeless and void—although that is definitely the kind of space God often shows up in. The kind of desert I'm talking about is the desert where we go off — or are taken off — to a place where it is just us and God, face-to-face, eye-to eye, heart-to-heart. It is a place where there is nothing to distract us, there is nowhere to run, nowhere to hide. It is a place where we find ourselves completely dependent on Him and there is no means of escape.

In the desert God has our undivided attention. In the desert God is our only means of survival. In the desert God is our only hope. That's why it is in the desert that God does some of his very best work; just ask Moses (Exodus 3), or Jacob (Genesis 32), or Elijah (1 Kings), or Jonah, or Paul (Galatians 1), or Jesus (Matthew 4). The desert creates a great environment for hearing God's voice. And the desert creates a great environment for convincing us that what he says is true, because everything else has been taken away and all we are left with is him.

In fact, it seems that the whole intent of the desert to begin with is to convince us of God's great affection. At least that's what it was all about in Hosea 2. In that particular passage God tells Hosea that he is going to take His unfaithful wife (Israel) into the desert. But the reason he wants to take her there is not at all what we would expect. *"Therefore I am now going to allure her; I will lead her into the desert and speak tenderly to her." (Hosea 2:14)* God is going to lead Israel into the desert to show his great heart for her, and to capture her heart with his great love. Somehow, in the desert, with no one or no thing around to distract her, God is going to woo her back to himself. He is going to *allure* her; which is a profoundly intimate word in the Hebrew that means *to open*. God is going to take her into the desert to open her so that he can enter into union with her in a way she could never imagine, but most deeply longs for.

The desert is the place where we are able to hear God in such a way that we actually become convinced of what he is saying to us. It is where true belief is formed.

Jesus and the Desert

The desert was a formative place in the life of Jesus. I don't pretend to understand even a little of what was really happening when the Spirit led Jesus into the desert to be tempted by Satan, but I do know that it was a tremendously significant event. It was significant because of what God said to Jesus just before he sent him there: *"This is my Son, whom I love: with him I am well pleased."* (Matthew 3:17) And it was significant because of how that affirmation came to life within Jesus and gave him ammunition to fight the enemy while he was in the desert. God the Father wanted those words ringing in the ears of his son as he struggled and was tempted. He wanted him to know that: *"You are my Beloved Son, whom I love, with you I am well pleased."* Knowing that truth to the depths of his being would help Jesus battle the voices of evil (*If you really are the son of God...*) that would try desperately to get him to believe something completely different than that. Jesus refused to listen to the voice of the deceiver and chose instead to be convinced of the truth uttered to him by the voice of his Father. The truth of his Father' love would set the tone not only for his time in the wilderness, but for his entire earthly ministry, sustaining him to and through the cross.

Brokenness

Another way that we can become convinced of God's great love and care is through brokenness. Brokenness is what occurs when our old ways are completely shattered — be it by events, by circumstances, or by chaos. Brokenness is when we are left with a bag full of pieces — that used to be our old life — trying to figure out what to do with it all. It is the place where we receive a new life, not necessarily by choice, but by necessity. Thus brokenness can be one of God's hardest, yet kindest gifts; we would not have let go of our old ways of being and seeing on our own, it had to be taken from us.

There are certain times, certain events, and certain places where whatever it is that God most deeply wants to do within us can be accomplished in no other way. Therefore brokenness becomes the avenue. And most often, it seems what God is most deeply trying to *get at* in times and places of brokenness are our beliefs; deconstructing the false narratives we have lived by and building some new, true, ones. Maybe we have subtly begun to believe that something other than God is the true source of life and happiness. Maybe we have come to believe in, or rely on, a certain set of circumstances that must exist in order for life to be worth living. Maybe we have subtly shifted from a life revolving around him alone, to a life revolving around Him *and* – or revolving around someone or something else altogether. Sometimes it is hard to tell.

But rest assured that when brokenness comes, there is some intention in the heart of God through it all. He very likely did not orchestrate the train wreck that happened, but He will use all things to mold us into the people and the followers that he longs for us to be. The beautiful truth of our faith is that regardless of the tragedy, God is always up to something – something redemptive and healing and formative. It all comes down to what we really believe about him. Do we really believe he is good…no matter what? If we do, then brokenness is something to embrace rather than to run from and avoid. Because, regardless of the pain and the heartache, brokenness is a gift. It grows belief within us.

Meditation

Blessed is the man
*   who walks not in the counsel of the wicked,*
nor stands in the way of sinners,
*   nor sits in the seat of scoffers;*
but his delight is in the law of the Lord,
*   and on his law he meditates day and night.*
He is like a tree
*   planted by streams of water*
that yields its fruit in its season,
*   and its leaf does not wither.*
In all that he does, he prospers. (Psalm 1:1-3)

One final, and a little more positive, way of becoming convinced of the truth of God's care, his character, and his love, is the practice of meditation. The word meditate comes from the Hebrew word *hagah*, which means to moan, mutter, or growl. It is the same word used in Isaiah 31:4 to describe a lion as it devours its prey. Therefore, meditation is a verbal, audible process.

It involves, in a sense, taking a word, or a phrase, or a verse, and chewing on it over and over and over again. Tasting and savoring every ounce of flavor that it has to offer. It is like eating a really great meal; the food tastes so good that you want to chew it for as long as possible before you actually have to swallow. And throughout the meal, you are verbally responding to just how good the food tastes.

I remember being with my wife on a trip one time and stopping to eat at one of our favorite restaurants in that particular city. It was a place we had been to a couple of times before and we were excited to visit again. And it certainly didn't disappoint. In fact, the food was so good that about all that came out of our mouths was: "Mmmmmm, Mmmmm, Mmmm! This food is soooo good! Have you tasted the…? Well it sure can't beat the…! Can you believe how good this food is?" We simply could not stop talking about it. That's just the way it is when we are completely captivated by something amazing.

That's the practice of meditation, come to life. We are captured, constantly repeating the word or phrase that God has given us to chew on, and doing so time after time after time. The repetition allows that word to sink so deeply into our hearts and souls that it becomes a part of us. As we continually repeat the word or phrase and focus all of our heart and energy upon it, it creates a wonderful space within us for the Spirit to move and to act. We somehow begin to become convinced of his goodness.

It's no accident that the Psalms tell us to "Taste and see that the Lord is good." (Psalm 34:8) The Psalms are actually full of encouragements to meditate on the Lord, as well as on his works and his love and his Law. By doing that something very good will happen both in the heart of God as well as in our own hearts and souls. The very first Psalm is a perfect example, telling us that the man is blessed who *meditates* on the Law of the Lord day and night. And not only is he blessed, he is fruitful. He becomes like a tree planted by streams of water — what an incredible image. When we meditate on the Law of the Lord, we *will* yield fruit; it is simply the result of planting ourselves in him and planting his Word in us. And not only will we yield fruit, but our leaf will not wither; and all that we do will prosper (which literally means *to go over or through*). What an incredible promise; all from practicing the art of meditation.

Practice

Select one of your favorite passages in scripture. Read it slowly and attentively a couple of times. Now pick one word, phrase, or image that somehow has stirred your heart and begin to meditate on it. Repeat it over and over, with your mouth and then with your heart. Chew on it. Taste it. Savor it. Continue to do this for ten minutes. Now stop and be quiet for a few minutes. What is going on in your heart and soul? Write about it in your journal.

Questions

What have you discovered about your beliefs as you read this chapter?

What does your life say about what you believe about God?

What false narratives (beliefs) must be deconstructed?

Where do you need to be, or long to be, convinced?

Chapter Five

Rest

rest [rest]: to be at ease, have tranquility or peace; to be quiet or still; refreshing ease; relief or freedom, especially from anything that wearies, troubles, or disturbs; a period or interval of inactivity, repose, solitude, or tranquility; mental or spiritual calm.

*"Let the beloved of the Lord **rest** secure in Him, for He shields him all day long, and the one the Lord loves **rests** between His shoulders. (Deuteronomy 33:12)*

*"In repentance and **rest** is your salvation, in quietness and trust is your strength...." (Isaiah 35:15)*

Years ago I had the privilege of being a part of a Spiritual Direction program at a seminary in the Seattle area. It was at a time in my life when God was doing some very intimate and wonderful things within me, and it provided such a rich and fruitful environment to nurture, encourage, and enable this new life of my soul to grow and flourish, as well as offering great time and space to reflect on it all. During the years that I was a part of this program, I had the incredible opportunity to sit under the teaching and influence of some of the most gifted, wise, and godly people I have ever met. Needless to say, it was a very formative time.

One of the classes I took was on the art of spiritual retreat. This class focused on the need for, and process of, going on retreat regularly — into silence and solitude. As a part of the class, we went on a day-long solitude retreat at a local convent. It was an incredible experience! The place was unbelievably beautiful; perched on a cliff, overlooking Puget Sound, on an absolutely gorgeous day. Seattle is a city usually known for its rainy weather, but on a sunny day, I am convinced, you will never see bluer blues and greener greens anywhere on earth. I guess that's why it is called the Emerald City.

The day was extraordinary: peaceful, quiet, refreshing, restful, and also quite challenging. At the end of the day we all gathered to reflect on, and talk about, our experience. And as we processed the day together, we were invited by our retreat facilitator to notice an ancient pattern that often shows itself in the spiritual life, particularly when one is on retreat. The last stage of this process is sometimes called *coming to rest,* or, as some of the saints of old might call it, *union.*

As we talked about this particular state of being, there was a wonderful recognition in us all that this is *the* place we all most deeply long to be. The only problem was, as one of my classmates said, "I don't know what to *do* when I get to that part." To which our retreat facilitator — a wonderfully feisty little nun from the convent — replied, "You don't *do* anything." That brought a perplexed look to the face of the young man who had asked the question, and a bit of a struggle as he tried to figure out how to word his next question without including the word *do.* "How...?" And that was as far as he got before this wise saint came up with words directly from the heart of God that impacted us all deeply. "This part of the process is like the silent embrace of two lovers," she gently and sweetly said. A hush fell over the room as we all let those words sink deeply into our hearts and souls. It was a sacred moment; a moment of clarity for us all; a kind of group *aha.*

As we all slowly filed out of the room I heard one guy quietly ask another, "What in the world does a nun know about the silent embrace of two lovers?" To which his friend wisely replied, "Who do you think her husband is? She probably knows that embrace far better than any of us." Truer words were likely never spoken.

Union

We all deeply long for just such an embrace. An embrace that lets us know to our core that we are both fully known and fully loved. An embrace that finally convinces us that our worth and value lies in the love-filled heart of the One who made us. An embrace that finally frees us from our frantic and desperate attempts at proving — to ourselves and to our world — that we are worth loving.

When we find ourselves in the passionate and peaceful arms of our Lover-God, we become truly convinced of our own belovedness. Then, and only then, are we able to experience the wholeness, the fullness, and the life that we were created for. Then, and only then, are we free to stop our grasping, clinging, striving, achieving, jockeying, proving, manufacturing, protecting, defending, and manipulating. Then, and only then, are we finally able to experience the *rest* that we so deeply long for.

Deuteronomy 33:12 says it so well: *"Let the beloved of the Lord rest secure in him, for He shields him all day long, and the one the Lord loves rests between His shoulders."* His love and affection, his strength and power, will hold us safely and securely. They will shield us and give us shelter from our deepest fears, anxieties, and insecurities. The word for *beloved* in this passage comes from the Hebrew root *dowd,* which means to boil. It is a word that is used over and over in the Song of Songs to describe an extremely passionate love. Thus, because of this truth — that we are fully, radically, and passionately loved — we are freed to lay our weary heads between the strong and loving shoulders of our Lover-God and find rest.

That is, in fact, the only way to find true and lasting rest in this chaotic and uncertain world, where there is far too much unknown, and far too much known. And that's just in the "outside world," there is also the whole world "inside," where we are filled with so many fears and doubts and insecurities. Who has a chance to find true rest in such a threatening climate? Only those whose rest doesn't depend on what we can create, or what we can achieve, or what we can avoid. Our safety and security must be dependent on something, or Someone, much bigger than we are. Someone big enough to calm our deepest fears and overcome our deepest insecurities. Someone with a heart we can trust and a hand we can be sure of. Someone who calls us Beloved and invites us to find our rest totally in him.

That is the invitation of God's embrace; an embrace that says to us: *"Are you tired? Worn out? Burned out on religion? Come to me. Get away with me and you'll recover your life. I'll show you how to take a real rest. Walk with me and work with me — watch how I do it. Learn the unforced rhythms of grace. I won't lay anything heavy or ill-fitting on you. Keep company with me and you'll learn to live freely and lightly."* (Matthew 11:28-30, The Message)

Find Rest, O My Soul

When we speak of *rest* in this context, we aren't just speaking of physical rest, we are speaking of something so much deeper and more substantial than that. This type of rest is a deep *soul rest*. Therefore, certain conditions and realities of the soul must be present to make it even a possibility. This type of rest is one that penetrates to our core, past our circumstances, to the very heart of our belief. It is only possible when we know to the core of our being that we are both fully known and fully loved by God. So, by its very nature, it cannot coexist with any type of striving or achieving or doing. It must involve simply *being* — freely being — present in the strong and loving embrace of our God.

Psalm 62 illustrates this well:

> *Find rest, O my soul, in God alone;*
> *my hope comes from Him.*
> *He alone is my rock and my salvation;*
> *He is my fortress, I will not be shaken.*
> *My salvation and my honor depend on God;*
> *he is my mighty rock, my refuge.*
> *Trust in Him at all times, O people;*
> *pour out your hearts to Him,*
> *for God is our refuge.*

*   *   *

> *One thing God has spoken,*
> *two things have I heard;*
> *that you, O God, are strong,*
> *and that you, O Lord, are loving.*
> *(Psalm 62:5-8, 11-12)*

In this Psalm, David is trying to show us that a certain pattern is at work for those of us who long to find rest for our weary souls. In fact, there is a progression in the Psalm that helps us understand what makes this type of rest possible. The Psalm acts as a kind of roadmap, if you will, telling us how we might arrive at this elusive destination. This road — to rest — first goes through trust and then travels all the way down into belief.

First David shows us that true rest depends on trust; not trust in our own circumstances, wealth, gifts, or abilities (or anyone else's), but trust in God *alone*. Until we are fully and completely willing and able to trust in his heart, his love, and his care for us, we will never find the rest for which we so deeply long.

Trusting in God *alone* can be a frightening proposition, however, because it means completely letting go of *all* of our own efforts and attempts at control. Only when we are trusting in God *alone* are we really trusting in God at all. It can never be God *and*, but only God *alone*. In the words of A. W. Tozer, "In the *and* comes our great woe." If I try to find rest in God *and* something or someone else, I am not really trying to find rest in God at all. True rest will not — and cannot — come from our own efforts, or our own achievements, or our own tenuous control over our lives and/or circumstances. If it depends on me — even a little bit — or on you, we are both in big trouble. For I will constantly fail, and you will constantly let me down. As a result, we will both live in constant fear, frustration, and insecurity; all of which are enemies of true rest.

David illustrates this so well when he writes, "*My salvation and my honor depend on God.*" Those responsibilities—salvation and honor—are two things that are far too big for me to control. If my salvation and my honor depend on me, I'll never find rest; I will be constantly working to try to assure those two things happen. I will be constantly working to try and earn my salvation, which is something that can never be earned. And I will be constantly working to achieve some level of honor, or glory for myself. The word *honor* in the Hebrew is the word *kabowb,* which comes from the verb *kabad*, which means *to be heavy or weighty.* In David's day, a thing's weight determined its value or worth. So if my value and worth depends on me, rest will never be an option; I will be constantly trying to justify my existence, to prove to myself and to my world that I am significant. True rest is only possible when both my salvation and my honor depend on God *alone.* He is the only one big enough, strong enough, and loving enough to have care of those two incredibly important conditions. Therefore I must learn to "*Trust in Him at all times.*" True rest requires complete trust.

But it doesn't just stop there. We must continue to go deeper into our hearts to confront the real issue—belief. What do we really believe to be true about God? Because ultimately, trust is dependent upon belief. That's the bottom line. And that's why the heart of this Psalm lies in verses 11-12: *One thing God has spoken, two things have I heard; that you, O God, are strong, and that you, O Lord, are loving.* What beautiful words and incredible truths. God is strong and

God is loving, and it is key that he is both of these at once. What good would it be to have a God who was loving but not strong? And how horrifying would it be to have a God who was strong, but not loving? In order for us to really trust Him, we must truly believe that He is both. We must believe to the core of our being that he is strong; able to care for us, defend us, redeem us, fight for us. And we must believe, in the deepest places of our hearts, that he is loving; that he loves us with a passionate, extravagant, and undying love. The Hebrew word used here for love is *chesed*, which means unfailing, unending, eternal love. Unless I truly believe that both of these things are true, I will never be able to trust in God, and, thus, never be able to find rest for my soul.

So the question becomes: *How does that type of belief become a reality?* I think part of the answer lies in the dialogue that Jesus has with Martha and Mary in Luke 10; a conversation that we have looked at already. We'll look at it in a little more detail below. But first, let me tell you a story.

One Thing

One evening, my wife and I were enjoying a quiet evening together at home. It had been a busy day and we had both changed into our comfy clothes, which says to the world, *"We're in for the night. Whatever happens in the world out there for the rest of the evening is just fine, but you guys will have to do without us. We're not coming back out."* It's the kind of feeling that makes you think, *I'm not sure how big the rocket would have to be to break me out of the gravitational pull of this house, and more particularly this couch, at this moment.*

In the midst of this comfortable state my wife turned to me with a horrible realization: we're out of coffee. Now, I'm not a coffee drinker, so for me this was not much of a crisis; definitely not enough to blast me out of the orbit of my house on this particular night. My wife, on the other hand, loves her morning coffee. And I love my wife. I also knew, in the way that only someone totally familiar with the language of a dearly loved one can, that she was asking me to brave the outer world and go to the grocery store to get coffee for the morning. So I slipped on my shoes, remaining in my comfy clothes — which, if any of our kids had been at home, would have driven them into all kinds of embarrassment — and headed to the grocery store on a mission to buy coffee.

As I entered the store, I began thinking to myself: *Hmmm, I'm kind of hungry. We didn't have any dessert tonight. I think I'd like to get a treat.* Which quickly led me down the ice cream aisle in pursuit of something to satisfy my sweet tooth. After I had perused the 1,000 different types of ice cream I was attracted to, I selected one and headed to the cash register. As I walked in that direction it occurred to me, *I'm out of shampoo, I need to go grab some while I'm here.* After grabbing the same kind of shampoo I've used for the past twenty years, I turned again toward the front of the store. Suddenly I was stopped by a deep-seated fear: *I think we're out of Diet Coke.* Now, if you really knew me, you would quickly realize how much of a problem that was for me.

Diet Coke is my coffee. So I turned toward the soft drink aisle, grabbed the Diet Coke and, once again, headed for the door.

As I was unloading the bags of treasure from my voyage onto the kitchen table back home, my wife looked at me and asked kindly, *"Where's the coffee?"* *Coffee*, I thought to myself. *Hmmm, coffee.* It seems that I had been sent out on a mission for *one thing* and, due to my own desires, my needs, and my fears, I had somehow gotten distracted and forgotten the *one thing* I had actually gone on that mission to get. Sound familiar?

If it doesn't sound familiar to you, it will definitely sound familiar when you read the story of Jesus' encounter with Martha and Mary in Luke 10:38-42. As you may recall, Martha had opened her home to Jesus and I'm sure was quite busy making sure everything looked just right; after all, if Jesus and his disciples were on their way to her house, so was the rest of the town—that's just the way life was wherever Jesus went. So there was lots to do. When Jesus arrived he found her in a bit of a frazzled state. In fact, the scriptures say that she was *distracted by all of the preparations that had to be made*. And not only was she frazzled, she was also frustrated; specifically, she was frustrated with her sister for not helping her. Somehow all of the many things that were going on—both within and around Martha—had distracted her from the point of it all: Jesus was in her house!

When she made her complaint to Jesus, he gently reminded her of this fact: *"Martha, Martha, you are worried and upset about many things, but few things are needed—or, indeed only one. Mary has chosen what is better and it will not be taken away from her."* Martha had become just like me in the grocery store, she had missed it. Somehow she had allowed the *many things* to distract her from the *one thing*. Somehow she had missed the *better* part.

I don't know why, but for some reason I always find myself defending Martha whenever I read this story. Maybe it is because I feel sorry for the criticism she endures from various religious circles. Maybe it is because I believe, or hope, she is simply misunderstood. Probably it is because I am really trying to defend, and feel okay about, my own Martha-like tendencies.

It is understandable, we live in a culture that values and applauds performance, productivity, and busyness. We live in a world that is all about getting things done. That is probably the reason why something always seems to rise up in me whenever this discussion rears its head. "Martha can't really help it," I tell myself, "that's just the way she's made, it's her personality." Through the years I have definitely adopted this line of thinking from time to time, but after reading and rereading this story — as well as others about these two sisters — I'm not so sure that's the case.

I wonder if Martha's behavior was more of a pattern, more a result of her paradigm than her personality. I wonder if Martha was really convinced of what Jesus was saying. I wonder if she really believed that what Mary was doing was *better*. Did she really believe that being with Jesus was the *one thing* that mattered? Or had she somehow convinced herself that the many things — how well she kept house, her reputation as a hostess, what people thought of her, getting things done, her own worries, fears and concerns — were somehow more important?

I really do not know, but I do want to at least ask the question. In fact, I need to ask the question. I need to ask the question not so much for Martha, but for myself. What do I believe is *better*? What do I believe is the *one thing* that really matters? The reason this is important is because I long to live a life of depth and quality. I want so much more in my life than simply running around like a chicken with my head cut off, reacting to whoever and whatever seems to be most urgent at the moment. I want a life focused on what is important instead of what is merely urgent. And I'll bet you do too.

Mary understood this. Instead of being consumed with all the things that had to get done, she was consumed with the *one thing* — Jesus. In the midst of all the chaos and the busyness and the distractions, her deepest desire was simply to sit at his feet and listen to what he said. That was what convinced her of his great love and affection. That was what completely captured her heart. That was the thing that was *better* than anyone or anything else. When he was around nothing else mattered, nothing else was important — only him. Listening to his voice is why her belief in him ran so deep, she knew his heart and therefore knew how deeply she was loved.

May it be the same for each of us. May we be like Mary. May we constantly find ourselves at his feet, looking into his eyes, and listening to his soft and tender voice. That is the *one thing.* That is what is *better.* It is really nothing more than prayer. And perhaps there is no better definition of prayer than that: just being with Him.

Contemplation

I've always had a sneaking suspicion that there is much more to most things than meets the eye — prayer being one of them. For years I was under the impression that prayer consisted of closing your eyes, bowing your head, and talking to God. The images of prayer that I carried around in my heart and mind left much to be desired. Prayer was not an activity I was particularly drawn to or excited about. My guess is that this had much more to do with my definition of prayer than it did with the real practice of prayer.

It wasn't until much later in life that I began to see that maybe my definition of prayer was far too small and rigid. Prayer isn't so much about performing a duty as it is about building a wonderfully intimate relationship. Prayer is not simply throwing all the words I can muster at the unseen God, but it — at its very core — has always been about union with the God who lives within us. That's what Jesus is really getting at in Matthew 6:5-8 when he talks about prayer. He's trying to recapture the true meaning and practice of prayer, which is simply being with God.

It is as if God himself (through the words of Matthew 6) is saying: *Don't stand on street corners, don't babble on and on; prayer is much more intimate and personal than that. Instead, go*

into your closet — that space where true intimacy is possible — and
shut the door. Leave everyone and everything else on the outside; I
want it to be just you and me. I want us to be together in a place
where I have your undivided attention. I have so much I want to
say to you; so much of me that I want you to know. And this space
and time is the place where that is most possible; the place where I
can have the deepest desires of my heart fulfilled, which is just to
be with you, my Beloved. Come inside where things are still and
quiet and you can hear every whisper of my loving Spirit deep
within your heart and soul. That's prayer.

Practice

Find a quiet place, where you will not be interrupted, and
settle into silence for a few minutes. After you have come to
some sense of stillness, simply sit in God's presence,
imagining yourself in his embrace. Resist all words that
might come; simply be with him, be held by him. Listen to
his heartbeat, look into his eyes, listen for his voice, know his
love. Do this for fifteen minutes. When you are finished,
thank him for the time and write about the experience in
your journal. Before you return to your daily life and
routine, schedule another time this week to do this very
same thing.

Questions

What is your reaction to the word rest?
When in your life have you experienced genuine rest?

What is the biggest obstacle in your life to rest?
What keeps you from resting in his loving embrace?
What does that reveal to you about your beliefs?

Chapter Six

Become

be come [bih-kuhm]: to come to be; come into being.

*Yet to all who received him, to those who believed in his name, he gave the right to **become** children of God. (John 1:12)*

Do not conform to the pattern of this world, but be transformed by the renewing of your mind. (Romans 12:2)

Spring is one of my favorite times of the year. The weather is warming, the breezes are blowing, and new life is beginning to "spring" up all around us. After the long, cold, colorless days of winter, spring reminds us that there is life and warmth and color within and underneath all things, just waiting for the right time to come forth. And when they do finally come forth, they seem to explode into being. This is true of my dogwoods and daffodils, my azaleas and rhododendron. Unfortunately, it is also true of my lawn.

Every spring I am reminded that it is time, once again, to begin the long season of mowing. Mowing is something that, at times, I actually enjoy. But it is winter that reminds me that, however much I might enjoy mowing my lawn at times, what I really enjoy is a long season of not having to do it. Each spring, as the grass begins to grow, I try to shake off the inertia of four to five months of mower inactivity.

First, I am not sure my mower is going to start, and, secondly, I am not really sure I want it to. Every spring, however, I venture into the garage and try to awaken my sleepy friend, wondering if I can coax him into roaring to life for one more season before I must lay him to rest in the lawn mower graveyard.

Once the mower actually starts, it is on to the front yard to begin the process of caring for that which is several days — if not weeks — late in needing attention. Let the mowing begin. At this point "mowing the lawn" might not be the most accurate description of what I am actually doing, mowing the weeds might be more fitting. In fact, during the first mowing of the season I wonder if there is a single blade of grass in my yard at all.

If you have a yard full of weeds there are several strategies you can adopt to remedy the situation: you can decide just to live with them; you can ignore them and hope they will go away; you can mow them short and try to make it look like they aren't there; or you can try to get rid of them completely. One interesting thing about weeds is that if you adopt the *cutting-them-short* strategy, you can actually make your yard look pretty good from a distance. You really can't tell the difference between the grass and the weeds — they're both green, right?

The problem is that weeds have a tendency to spread and, if you allow them to do so, they will take over your entire yard, leaving the grass no room to grow. Therefore something needs to be done to eliminate the weeds entirely; they have to die in order to make fruitful space in which the grass can live. If you just deal with the problem at a surface level, you are fighting a losing battle; the weeds will grow right back with a vengeance. You must go all the way to the root of the problem.

It is the same way with the life of the Spirit. In our longing for true and lasting change in our lives, we often try to treat our "weeds" at a surface level rather than going all the way down to the root issues. And that's perfectly understandable, it's a lot easier to cut off the weed at the surface than it is to uproot it. Uprooting takes time and effort, and is a long and often painful process. The problem is that if we want genuine transformation in our lives, it will only come when we begin to recognize and attack the root of the problem.

Paul talks about this in Romans 6:6 when he writes: *For we know that our old self was crucified with him so that the body of sin might be done away with, that we should no longer be slaves to sin — because anyone who has died has been freed from sin.* If we try to eliminate sin at a surface level — that is, just trying to crucify a certain behavior rather than uprooting the cause of the behavior — then we are fighting a losing battle. Our sin will simply grow right back because we haven't attacked the root. There is a much larger story underneath; a story that needs to be identified, confessed, and repented of. That larger story is about the false (or, as Paul calls it, *old*) self we have created, or that has been created for us by living in a fallen and broken world. Until we deal with the root issue — the false story — true and lasting change will only be an illusion.

Conformed and Transformed

In Romans 12:2, Paul uses two really helpful words in talking about this process. First he says; "*Do not conform any longer to the pattern of this world.*" The word used here, *syschematizo*, means *to fashion oneself according to*. It conveys the idea of forming ourselves into the image of that which is around us. The J. B. Philips translation of this verse says, "*Don't let the world around you squeeze you into its own mould.*" But that is not completely accurate, because this conforming is not something simply *done to us* that we have no control over, it is something *done by us*. This process is far more active on our part than we would like to admit. We actively form ourselves into the image of the world around us. It is our doing. And Paul says, "Do not do this any longer."

Paul goes on to say: *"But be transformed by the renewing of your mind."* The word transformed is *metamorphoo*, which means to change into another form altogether. It is where we get the word *metamorphosis*, as in the change than takes place when a caterpillar turns into a butterfly.

Notice the contrast between *do not conform* and <u>be</u> *transformed*. The process of transformation is not one we can manipulate and control, but one we can only surrender to; a process that happens by *the renewing of our minds*. Once we recognize and stop living according to our old/false self, and begin to believe the truth of the true/new self that has been bestowed upon us by God, then we will *become* new creations. Here's a story that helps illustrate this point.

Trying

Continuing with the mowing metaphor, last spring I got my lawn mower stuck in the mud in my back yard. Well, it actually wasn't me, and it wasn't actually my lawn mower, but that's a longer story. Anyway, it was stuck in a ditch in the back of the yard where the pond drains out into a creek that runs behind our property. It was stuck good too; the tires were half way buried in the mud. Three people pushing still couldn't get it out; in fact, the harder we tried, the deeper it sank.

Have you ever felt like that? Like the harder you try to extricate yourself from those broken and hurtful patterns of the "false self" way of thinking—the harder you try to get yourself *out of the mud*—the deeper you seem to sink? It is like when you *try* to rest. Or when you *try* to go to sleep. Or you *try* to be still inside. The *trying* seems to make it less and less of a real possibility. Or when you *try* not to worry or not to think about something in particular. It seems like the more effort and energy you focus on the problem, the deeper it seems to get. Maybe that's why Paul tells us in Philippians 4:6 not to worry, but instead to pray. The peace of God *which surpasses all understanding* enters the picture only as a result of praying—letting go of worry and holding on to God.

Maybe that's why a little later on Paul tells us, "Finally, brothers and sisters, whatever is true, whatever is noble, whatever is right, whatever is pure, whatever is lovely, whatever is admirable—if anything is excellent or praiseworthy—think about such things. Whatever you have learned or received or heard from me, or seen in me—put it into practice. And the God of peace will be with you." (Philippians 4:8-9) Get it? This is how we go about *renewing our minds*. Peace comes not when our hearts and thoughts are consumed with the problem, but when they are consumed with that which is wonderful, excellent, and praiseworthy—with God himself.

Years ago I had a friend who made the Olympic Team in the 100-meter hurdles. I mean this guy could run—and still can, although he is now in his early fifties. Once I asked him how he was able to run the hurdles so fast and, seemingly, so effortlessly. He talked about practice, preparation, and working hard at it, but he also talked about how the movements became so familiar and natural to him over time. He was actually able to knock a quarter that had been placed on the top of each hurdle off of the hurdle with his leg without touching the hurdle itself. Is that not amazing? I told him that if I tried that, I would kill myself hitting the hurdle. He said, "You can't focus on the hurdle, you have to focus on the finish line. If you focus on the hurdle, you hit the hurdle." To this day I remember that little piece of wisdom because it is not only true on the track, but also in life. If we are consumed by the hurdles, we will never get over them; they will only seem to grow larger and larger. We must keep our eyes focused on the *good part* — that which is *excellent*, i.e., on the finish line — on Jesus (see Hebrews 12:1-2).

Maybe that's why David counsels us in Psalm 37:1-4 *not to fret*, but to: "[t]rust in the Lord and do good; dwell in the land and enjoy safe pasture. Take delight in the Lord, and he will give you the desires of your heart." (Psalm 37:1-4) He says a little later on "do not fret — it leads only to evil." The dictionary definition of the word *fret* is *to feel or express worry, annoyance, discontent, or the like,* or *to cause corrosion; gnaw into something.* In other words, fretting is a consuming activity. Don't do it! Instead, be consumed with that which is beautiful — God. Trust in Him! Delight in Him! That will change you.

Anyway, the lawn mower would not budge. We could do nothing, in and of ourselves, to get it out. We would have to rely on something bigger and stronger to pull it out. So we drove a four-by-four truck into the back yard, tied a rope to the mower, and pulled it out. In order to do this, the mower had to be *attached* to the truck. Interestingly the Hebrew word for *trust* comes from the root meaning *to attach.* Of course it does.

So what is it exactly that I'm trying to say? What I'm trying to say is that when we get consumed with the *doing* of something, sometimes that actually hinders rather than helps that certain something *become* a reality. Sometimes the harder we *try,* the more stuck we get.

When we are trying to change these destructive life patterns, maybe we need to focus our attention and our affection and our efforts on the beauty and character and majesty of God instead of on whatever we are trying to solve or correct or conquer. Maybe what we really need to do, is to fall hopelessly in love with Jesus, and leave the rest up to him. As we *become* more and more consumed with him, we will be more and more captured by the vision that we see. And then, as Paul put it so beautifully, we will be transformed into that very image: *"We all, with unveiled face, beholding the glory of the Lord, are being transformed into the same image from one degree of glory to another."* (2 Corinthians 3:18)

Push and Pull

There are two significant forces always at work in the process of spiritual transformation: there is a push and there is a pull. Both are vital components of the process, but often they are separated from one another rather than held together the way they need to be. To our detriment, when they are separated, our tendency is to fly off in one direction, at the expense of the other.

First, in the process of change, there must always be a *push*. The push is the part of the process where we realize that we have fallen far short of what we were created and intended to be. The push is the recognition of our utter sinfulness and our desperate need for a Savior. The gospel of John uses the word conviction: *"When the Counselor comes, he will convict the world of guilt in regard to sin and righteousness and judgment." (John 16:8)* In this way the Spirit convicts us of our propensity to continually go our own way in defiance of, and disobedience to, the God who created us. The energy behind this conviction is a sense of guilt and shame that is used as a means of pushing us towards God. Push involves a deep, deep recognition of our immense and overwhelming need.

But there is another part to this story, there is another movement in this process. There is also a *pull*. This pull involves not so much an awareness of our immense need, as an awareness of his immense love. The pull involves being completely captured, and captivated, and allured, and overwhelmed by his intimate, passionate, and undying love.

The pull is what God talks about in Hosea when he says of Israel, his wayward bride, *"Therefore I am now going to allure her; I will lead her into the wilderness and speak tenderly to her."* *(Hosea 2:14)*

I have the privilege of teaching a spiritual formation class each semester with a group of college students. It is a time that I dearly love, as I watch these young men and women dig into some of these issues. In one class a couple of years ago, as we were talking about this process of push and pull, I mentioned that the most transformational times in my life have occurred when God grabbed hold of my heart and intimately and passionately pulled me to himself. I used the word *romancing*; that God is continually transforming me by romancing me, and that he, in turn, is bent on romancing them into transformation as well. As others in the class began to discuss that image, one of the girls spoke up with a blush and said, "He has romanced me so much already, if He romances me any more I just don't know if I can stand it."

She got it. She understood the *pull* of the Lover God who longs for a passionate intimacy with her that will change everything about her. Because, at its core, spiritual transformation is about falling in love with God. That is how we *become*.

Putting it All Together

So *becoming* is not so much something we do, as it is the end result of what God is doing in us. Becoming, by definition, has a whole lot more to do with being than it does with doing: being aware of his voice, being open to his hand, and being convinced of his love. Those are the things that, in the end, transform us.

Becoming involves *recognizing* the things we have believed through the years about God and about ourselves that are simply not true and allowing the voice of God to speak against them. Then it involves deconstructing and *releasing* those false beliefs and narratives — as well as the patterns, habits and behaviors that have come about as a result of them — and giving them totally to God. It involves *receiving* the new self, this identity that God bestows upon us, and actually *believing* that it is true. Finally, it involves *resting* in the beauty of that truth. Once we are actually convinced of the truth of who we are in him, his Beloved, the end result is that we *become* more and more like him. Thanks be to God!

Practice

Make some space in your life to spend at least an hour, if not more, with God. Start with silence and allow your heart to settle and become fully present to him. Now, in your journal, write down each of the six words that begin a chapter. Take each word individually and just spend some time listening to God about that particular word. What does that word reveal in you? What does it do in you? What is his invitation to you? Write whatever thoughts or stirrings of the Spirit that he brings to mind during that time. After you have spent time with each word, spend some time considering them all in relation to each other. What does God bring to your mind or heart? What is he saying to you? Thank him for his love and presence, and then spend some time in prayer.

Questions

What is the most formative thing in your life these days?
How are you allowing that thing to form you?
What is God up to within you these days?
How is he transforming you?
What does the word *become* do within you?
When you think of *becoming,* what do you dream about?

Conclusion

They are two conversations that I will remember for a long, long time. The first was with a friend sitting over breakfast at a local restaurant one morning. We had both been assaulted by a season's worth of busyness, hurry and chaos, and during the conversation a question arose. I'm not really sure who asked it, in fact, maybe it asked itself.

Wherever it came from, or more probably *Whoever* it came from, it ended up on the table between us. *Are you living the life you really want to live?* It is a question that needs to be understood before it can be answered. The essence of the question has nothing to do with houses and cars and money, or even success and ease and comfort. At its core it is a question about the inner quality of our lives: the life of God living inside of us and how that expresses itself in the significant relationships in our lives. Maybe a more accurate way of asking the question is: *"Are you living the life God wants to live in and through you?"* And if not, why not?

So there it was, on the table for us to answer. And I don't remember exactly what my answer was on that particular morning, but I do vividly remember the deep, rich conversation that followed. I remember the part where we dreamt together about what *that life* really looks like. It made me come alive inside.

The second conversation was actually seven or so years earlier. I was sitting at lunch with a dear friend who had recently been diagnosed with cancer and told that he had roughly three months to live. I remember asking him what it felt like to hear those words, and what was going on inside of him as a result. His answer amazed me. He said that he had always imagined that when he heard those words that he would immediately start making a list of all the things he wanted to do and the people he needed to see before his time was up. "*But,*" he said, "*That's not the way it was at all. As a matter of fact, what I found out was that I had been living the life I most wanted to live.*"

He had lived a life of depth and quality with his family, with his friends, in his work, and, most of all, with his God. He had lived a life of majoring on the majors; of being about the things that he and, most importantly, God most wanted to be about. There were no regrets, there was no frenzy, no long list—just peace. What an incredibly powerful statement! Needless to say, I was deeply impacted, both challenged and overwhelmed.

How do we go about living the life that we most deeply long to live? How do we live a life of depth and quality with God, which will lead to a life of depth and quality with our families and our friends and our world? It doesn't just happen, say the saints and the poets, it takes some reflection and intention and desire. "*We fool ourselves if we think that such a sacramental way of living is automatic,*" Richard Foster once wrote. "*This kind of living communion does not just fall on our heads. We must desire it and seek it out. We must order our lives in particular ways.*"

Call it Christian practice, call it spiritual disciplines, or call it means of grace, but somehow we have to prayerfully consider how to move in the direction of the life we think God most wants to live in us. The church fathers called that *somehow* a Rule of Life. St. Benedict's rule is the most famous example. It involves identifying what we most want our lives to be about—in St. Benedict's case, prayer—and then figuring out, as best we can, how we will move in the direction of making that life a possibility; creating space and time for that life to be able to happen. The *happening* of it is ultimately up to God, but making the space and the time is our part. We must listen and pray and plan and order our lives in certain ways, so that at the end of our days we don't find ourselves wondering how we've somehow missed it.

St. Benedict wrote a *rule* to order his life, and the life of his community, around the practice of prayer; in his heart and soul he knew that everything else must revolve around that. *Everything else* would involve the things that were necessary to make a life of prayer possible: in order to pray we must eat, and in order to eat we must work, and in order to work we must rest, all in order that we might pray. A holistic approach to life for sure—spiritual, physical, vocational, and relational. His rule became the simple rhythm that his community lived by.

If we are serious about living the life we most deeply long to live, it must be the same for us. It won't just fall on our heads either. We must begin to live our lives purposefully and intentionally. What is the old adage? *"If you aim at nothing, you'll hit it every time."* We must begin to live by a thoughtful and prayerful *rule* as well. (In actuality, we all live by a *rule* whether we realize it or not.)

To create this Rule of Life—in the words of my friend Robert Benson, "the Rule of Whatever Your Name May Be"—we must listen and reflect and dream with God about the life we most deeply long to live, or the life He most deeply longs to live in us. Once we begin to get a vision of what that life looks like, we must begin to reflect on the life we are currently living and ask, "*What am I currently doing that is fruitfully moving me in the direct of the life I long to live in Christ? And what am I currently doing that is not moving me fruitfully in that direction?*"

In the words of Robert Benson once again: "*Only by taking our life apart from time to time and examining it carefully, and then putting it back together thoughtfully and prayerfully, only then can we have some measure of confidence that we are living the life that we were meant to lead.*"

After recognizing the fruitful and unfruitful parts of our current "practice," then we must begin to ask God, and dream about, what things, or practices, or disciplines, or means of grace might actually help make space for the life he longs to live in us. We must begin to consider how to make those things a part of our daily routine. What will I do daily? What will I do weekly? What will I do monthly? And what will I do yearly? All are questions we ask in the name of making space for God to speak, and to move, and to act. And we also must ask questions like: What is the fruit that I seek from this Rule? Who will hold me accountable? And when will I reflect and re-evaluate?

In this way, your Rule of Life, the life you most deeply long to live, *comes into being.* Thanks be to God!

Thanks

Special thanks to all of the saints and artists, poets and pilgrims who have spoken into my life through the years, I am forever in your debt. Somehow, through listening to your voices, I have found my own. And special thanks to my family: Carol, Tim, Michelle, and Hunter. I love you more than words can possibly express! And special thanks to Paige, for taking a bunch of words and helping shape them into something that looks more like a work of art. The kind offering of your gifts has made this book so much better than it ever could've been without you. And finally, special thanks to you, for reading. Your investment of time and energy and attention is a gift that I do not take for granted. I hope it was worth it.

Other books available on Amazon.com:

Beginnings
Being with Jesus
Pieces
Reflections

Or follow my blogs:

bluebookblog: jb-bluebookblog.blogspot.com
Room to Flourish: jb-coreleadership.blogspot.com

21632051R00067

Made in the USA
San Bernardino, CA
30 May 2015